BRUCE NORRIS

Bruce Norris's other plays include *A Parallelogram*, *The Unmentionables*, *The Pain and the Itch*, *We All Went Down to Amsterdam*, *Purple Heart* and *The Infidel*. His work has been produced at the Royal Court Theatre (London), Playwrights Horizons (New York), Steppenwolf Theatre and Lookingglass Theatre (Chicago), Philadelphia Theatre Company, Woolly Mammoth Theatre (Washington DC), Staatstheater Mainz (Germany) and the Galway Festival (Ireland), among others.

He is the recipient of the Steinberg Playwright Award (2009), and the Whiting Foundation Prize for Drama (2006), as well as two Joseph Jefferson Awards (Chicago) for Best New Work. As an actor he can be seen in the films *A Civil Action*, *The Sixth Sense* and *All Good Things*. He lives in New York.

Bruce Norris

CLYBOURNE PARK

NICK HERN BOOKS
London
www.nickhernbooks.co.uk

A Nick Hern Book

Clybourne Park first published in Great Britain as a paperback original in 2010 by Nick Hern Books Limited, 14 Larden Road, London W3 7ST, in association with the Royal Court Theatre, London

Reprinted with a new cover in 2011

Clybourne Park copyright © 2010, 2011 Bruce Norris

Bruce Norris has asserted his right to be identified as the author of this work

Cover image: aka
Cover design: Ned Hoste, 2H

Typeset by Nick Hern Books, London
Printed and bound in Great Britain by CPI Bookmarque, Croydon, Surrey

A CIP catalogue record for this book is available from the British Library

ISBN 978 1 84842 178 3

Clybourne Park received its West End premiere at the Wyndham's Theatre, London, on 8 February 2011 (previews from 28 January), with the following cast:

RUSS/DAN	Stuart McQuarrie
BEV/KATHY	Sophie Thompson
FRANCINE/LENA	Lorna Brown
JIM/TOM	Sam Spruell
ALBERT/KEVIN	Lucian Msamati
KARL/STEVE	Stephen Campbell Moore
BETSY/LINDSEY	Sarah Goldberg
KENNETH	Michael Goldsmith

Director	Dominic Cooke
Set and Costume Designer	Robert Innes Hopkins
Lighting Designer	Paule Constable
Sound Designer	David McSeveney

It was produced by Royal Court Theatre Productions, Sonia Friedman Productions, Old Vic Productions and Eric Abraham.

This production was first performed at the Royal Court, Jerwood Theatre Downstairs, London, on 2 September 2010 (previews from 26 August), with the following cast:

RUSS/DAN	Steffan Rhodri
BEV/KATHY	Sophie Thompson
FRANCINE/LENA	Lorna Brown
JIM/TOM	Sam Spruell
ALBERT/KEVIN	Lucian Msamati
KARL/STEVE	Martin Freeman
BETSY/LINDSEY	Sarah Goldberg
KENNETH	Michael Goldsmith

Clybourne Park received its world premiere at Playwrights Horizons, New York, on 21 February 2010, with the following cast:

RUSS/DAN	Frank Wood
BEV/KATHY	Christina Kirk
FRANCINE/LENA	Crystal A. Dickinson
JIM/TOM/KENNETH	Brendan Griffin
ALBERT/KEVIN	Damon Gupton
KARL/STEVE	Jeremy Shamos
BETSY/LINDSEY	Annie Parisse

Director	Pam MacKinnon
Set Designer	Daniel Ostling
Costume Designer	Ilona Somogyi
Lighting Designer	Allen Lee Hughes
Sound Designer	John Gromada
Production Stage Manager	C. A. Clark

| *Artistic Director* | Tim Sanford |
| *General Manager* | Carol Fishman |

For Frances Watson

Characters

ACT ONE (1959)

RUSS, *white, late forties*
BEV, *white, married to Russ, forties*
FRANCINE, *black, thirties*
JIM, *white, late twenties*
ALBERT, *black, married to Francine, thirties*
KARL, *white, thirties*
BETSY, *married to Karl, late twenties*

ACT TWO (2009)

TOM, *played by the actor who plays Jim*
LINDSEY, *played by the actor who plays Betsy*
KATHY, *played by the actor who plays Bev*
STEVE, *married to Lindsey, played by the actor who plays Karl*
LENA, *played by the actor who plays Francine*
KEVIN, *married to Lena, played by the actor who plays Albert*
DAN, *played by the actor who plays Russ*
KENNETH

The set is the interior of a modest three-bedroom bungalow, 406 Clybourne Street, in the near north-west of central Chicago. There is a sitting room with front-door access, a fireplace with an oak mantelpiece, and a separate dining area with built-in cupboards. At the rear of the dining area, a swinging door leads to a kitchen. A staircase leads up to a second floor, and beneath it, another door leads down to a basement. There is a hallway and a bathroom door as well.

ACT ONE

September, 1959. Three o'clock, Saturday afternoon. The house is in disarray. Cardboard boxes are stacked in corners. Some furniture has been removed, shelves emptied. Pictures have been removed from the walls, and carpets have been rolled and stood on end. Not far from the fireplace, RUSS sits alone reading a copy of National Geographic. *He is dressed in pyjama top and chinos, socks, no shoes. On a table next to him sits a carton of ice cream into which, from time to time, he dips a spoon. Music plays softly on his transistor radio.*

After a moment, BEV descends the stairs carrying linens which she will add to a cardboard box. As she does she stops to look at RUSS.

BEV. You're not going to eat all of that, are you?

He turns down the radio.

RUSS (*with his mouth full*). Whaddya say?

BEV. What ice cream is that?

RUSS. Um. (*Looks at the carton.*) Neapolitan.

BEV. Well, don't feel compelled to eat that.

RUSS (*shrugs, barely audible*). Going to waste.

He turns the radio back up and BEV crosses to the dining room. FRANCINE enters from the kitchen, wearing a maid's uniform. RUSS remains in the foreground as we overhear:

FRANCINE (*to BEV*). So, if it's all right, I'm just going to put these candlesticks here in the big box with the utensils.

BEV. That is what I would do, yes, but you do mean to wrap them first?

FRANCINE. Oh, yes, ma'am.

BEV. Oh. Now, Francine: I was wondering about this chafing dish, which we have practically never used.

FRANCINE. Yes, ma'am.

BEV. Do you own one of these yourself?

FRANCINE. No, I sure don't.

BEV. Because I do love to entertain, though for the life of me I can't remember the last time we did. But still, it does seem a shame to give it away because it's just such a nice thing, isn't it?

FRANCINE. Oh, yes it is.

BEV. And it just looks so lonely sitting there in the cupboard *so*: I was wondering if this might be the sort of thing that would be useful to you?

FRANCINE. Ohhhh, thank you, I couldn't take that.

BEV (*re: chafing dish*). See how sad he looks?

FRANCINE. You don't want to be giving that to me.

BEV. Well, nonetheless, I'm offering.

FRANCINE. No, I don't think I should.

BEV. Well, you think about it.

FRANCINE. But thank you for offering.

BEV. You think about it and let me know.

FRANCINE. Yes, ma'am.

BEV. And do put some paper around those.

FRANCINE. Yes, ma'am.

> FRANCINE *goes into the kitchen.* BEV *continues to pack, passing* RUSS.

BEV. That's a funny word, isn't it? Neapolitan.

RUSS (*turns off radio*). Funny what way?

BEV. What do you suppose is the origin of that?

RUSS. Uhhh… Naples, I imagine.

BEV. *Naples?*

RUSS. City of Naples?

BEV. Noooo.

RUSS. Of or pertaining to.

BEV. That would not be my first guess.

RUSS. Yup.

BEV. *I* would think it had something to do with *neo*, as in something *new*, and then there's the *-politan* part which to me would suggest a *city*, like *metropolitan*.

RUSS. Could be.

BEV. Meaning *new city* or something to that effect.

RUSS (*shrugs*). Told you what *I* think.

BEV. Because a person from Naples, I mean they wouldn't be called, well, not *Napoleon*, obviously. I guess that was already taken! (*Laughs, then serious.*) On the other hand, you *do* say *Italian*. But *cities*, though, and specifically ones that end in S, because there must be a rule of some sort, don't you think? Help me think of a city other than *Naples* that also ends in S?

Pause.

RUSS. Uhhh –

BEV. Oh fiddle. Um.

RUSS. Des Moines.

BEV. Not a *silent* S.

RUSS. Brussels.

BEV. All right. There you go. And how do we refer to them?

RUSS. Belgians.

BEV. But, the people from the *city*.

RUSS. Never *met* anyone from Brussels.

BEV. But there has to be a word.

RUSS. Look it up.

BEV. Where?

RUSS. Dictionary?

BEV. But it's not going to say this is the capital of Belgium and
by the way the people who live there are called –

RUSS. Give Sally a call.

BEV. She won't know that.

RUSS. She and Ray went to Paris.

BEV. So?

RUSS. *Close* to Brussels.

BEV. Sally never knows those sort of things.

RUSS. Oh. Oh.

BEV. What?

RUSS. Parisians.

BEV. What about them?

    FRANCINE *returns with more packing*.

RUSS. Paris ends in S.

BEV. But – It's not Brusselsians.

RUSS. Or Nice.

BEV. I'm serious.

RUSS. Got the S *sound*.

BEV. But not *Nicians*. Like *Grecians*.

RUSS. No, no. *Niçoise*.

BEV. I know that, but –

RUSS. Know that salad your sister makes?

BEV. But that's *French* –

RUSS. It's a French *city*.

BEV. I understand, but, I'm saying how would we say, in
Eng – ? Well, now I don't remember the original question.

RUSS. Brussels.

BEV. No no.

RUSS. Des Moines?

BEV. *No*.

RUSS. Naples.

BEV. *Naples*. And I don't think *Neapolitan*. How would that become *Neapolitan*?

RUSS. Muscovites.

BEV. What?

RUSS. People from Moscow.

BEV. Well, I give up, because that's just *peculiar*.

RUSS (*chuckles at the word*). *Muscovites*.

BEV (*the same*). I wonder if they're *musky*.

RUSS (*savouring the sound*). *Musss-covites*.

BEV (*coming up with one*). Cairenes!

RUSS. *That* is a strange one.

BEV. I'm telling you, that's what they're called!

RUSS. I'm not disputing.

BEV. But why *Cairenes*?

RUSS (*shrugs*). Dated a girl named *Irene*.

FRANCINE *exits again*.

BEV. Or Congolese?

RUSS. That, too, is correct.

BEV. So why don't we say *Tongalese*?

RUSS. Or *Mongolese*.

BEV. No, Mongol-*oid*.

RUSS. No no, that's different.

BEV (*aghast at her own faux pas*). Oh, you're right.

RUSS. That's uhhh, you know, that's –

BEV. No, I know.

RUSS (*gestures toward his brain*). The thing with the –

BEV. Like the Wheeler boy.

RUSS. Right. The one who –

BEV. Bags the groceries.

RUSS. Right.

Beat, then:

BEV. But that's nice, isn't it, in a way? To know we all have our place.

RUSS. There but for the grace of God.

BEV. Exactly.

Pause. RUSS *breaks it with:*

RUSS (*pronouncing grandly, with a sweep of his hand*). Ulan Bator!

BEV. What?

RUSS (*an exact repeat*). Ulan Bator!

BEV. What are you doing?

RUSS (*once again*). Ulan – !

BEV. Stop it. Tell me what you're doing.

RUSS. Capital of Mongolia.

BEV. Well, why would I know that?

RUSS (*shrugs*). *National Geographic*.

BEV. Oh oh. Did you change the address like I asked you?

RUSS. What do you mean?

BEV. For the *National Geographic*.

RUSS. The address?

BEV. Oh, *Russ*!

RUSS. Me?

BEV. I *asked* you.

RUSS. You did?

BEV. I asked you *fifteen* times.

RUSS. When?

BEV. I said don't forget the change of address for the magazine and you promised me that you would, you promised me *specifically* – (*Continues*.)

RUSS (*overlapping*). I did it last week.

BEV. – that you would see to it so I – Oh.

RUSS. Pulling your leg.

BEV. I see.

RUSS (*a gentle imitation*). Oh *Russ*!!

BEV. Maybe people don't *like* having their leg pulled.

RUSS. I was just – I was – Okay.

> *Pause.*

BEV. And are you going to bring that trunk down from upstairs?

RUSS. Yup.

BEV. Thought you said after lunch.

RUSS. Sort of a two-person job.

BEV. And you really want to wear those clothes all day?

RUSS. Hadn't really thought about it.

> *A silence passes between them.* RUSS *scratches his elbow.*

BEV. But you know, you *are* a funny person. I was telling Francine – I ran into Barbara Buckley at Lewis and Coker's and Barbara said that Newland told her a funny joke that you told at Rotary last year.

RUSS. That *I* told?

BEV. About a man with a talking dog?

RUSS (*shakes his head*). Thinking of Don Lassiter.

BEV. No, it was you.

RUSS. Don's the one with the jokes.

BEV. You know jokes. You tell jokes.

RUSS. A talking *dog*?

BEV. And Barbara said does Russ not go to Rotary any more? Apparently they all keep saying where's Russ? (*A beat, then:*) Not that I care one way or the other but it does seem that you used to enjoy going and I don't see why that, of all things, should have to change –

RUSS *shifts in his chair.*

(*Quickly.*) – and please don't say *what's the point*, Russ. I hate it when you say that. Because for that matter – (*Continues.*)

RUSS (*overlapping*). I wasn't going to say –

BEV. – what's the point of *anything* enjoyable, really? –

Phone rings. FRANCINE *enters.*

Why not just sit in a chair all day and wait for the end of the world but *I* don't intend to live the remainder of my life like that and I think you could take notice of the fact that talking that way *frightens* me.

FRANCINE (*answering phone*). Stoller residence?

RUSS (*quietly, to* BEV). Not trying to frighten you.

FRANCINE (*on phone*). Who may I say is calling, please?

RUSS (*to* BEV, *quietly*). Ulan Bator.

FRANCINE. Excuse me, Miz Stoller?

BEV. Who is it?

FRANCINE. Mr Lindner wanting to talk to you.

RUSS (*with a groan*). Ohh for the love of –

BEV (*to* FRANCINE). Tell him I'll call him back.

RUSS. Not one thing it's another.

FRANCINE (*on phone*). Mr Linder, she wonders if she can call you back?

BEV (*to* RUSS). I only mean that people are concerned about you – (*Continues.*)

RUSS (*overlapping*). Well, what's the *nature* of the concern?

BEV. – and I don't see the point of spurning their good intentions.

RUSS. Gee whiz, I'm just reading a magazine.

FRANCINE (*to* BEV). Says he's calling from a payphone.

RUSS (*to* FRANCINE). Just say we're occupied.

BEV. No, I'll take it, thank you, Francine. (*To* RUSS, *as she crosses*.) I'm just repeating what Barbara said. (*On phone.*) Hello?

RUSS (*to himself*). Barely know the woman.

BEV (*on phone*). No no no, it's just, we're in a state of disarray, Karl.

RUSS. Somehow I *spurned* her.

As FRANCINE *returns to the kitchen, the front door opens and* JIM *sticks his head in. He is a youthful minister – wears a clerical collar under his jacket.*

JIM. Ding dong?

RUSS (*seeing* JIM, *not rising*). Oh. Uh, hey, Bev?

JIM. May one intrude, he politely asked?

RUSS (*to* BEV). Jim's at the door.

BEV (*seeing* JIM, *she mouths silently to him*). Oh, oh, oh! *Come in!! Come in!!* (*On phone.*) Karl, I can't hear what you're saying.

JIM. Russ, my friend, I am crossing the threshold!

RUSS. Hey, Jim.

JIM (*looking around*). Holy Toledo Jiminy Christmas.

RUSS. Bev's on the phone.

JIM. Hate to be the one to break it to ya, buddy, but somebody made off with yer stuff!

RUSS. Kinda discombobulated.

BEV (*on phone*). Oh, Karl, I don't think so, not today.

JIM (*to* RUSS). S'not the big day, is it?

RUSS (*to* JIM). No no. Monday.

BEV (*on phone*). No, it's just, Russ is a little under the weather.

JIM. Piece of advice. Watch out when you start lifting things. Learned that the hard way last month.

RUSS (*preoccupied with* BEV). Izzat right?

JIM (*to* RUSS). Ohhhh *yeah*. Judy says Jim, I gotta have me this spinet piano, a task which naturally falls to *me* – (*Continues.*)

BEV (*on phone, overlapping*). Well, if it's absolutely necessary.

JIM. – and there I am with this thing halfway up the front steps and me *underneath*. And, of course, it's not the *weight*, you know. It's the *angle* – (*Continues.*)

BEV. All right, Karl. (*Hangs up.*)

JIM. – which is why they tell ya to bend the knees.

BEV (*re:* JIM). Well, will you look what the cat dragged in?

RUSS (*to* BEV, *re: the phone call*). What was that about?

JIM. Bev, I am *trying* to bestow the pearls of my wisdom upon this man.

RUSS (*to* JIM). No no, I was listening.

BEV. Oh, isn't it just a *jumble* in here, all of this?

JIM. S'what I was saying to Russ, said somebody cleaned ya out!

RUSS. Not coming here, is he?

BEV. Oh, I don't know. You know Karl.

JIM. Karl Lindner?

RUSS. Bev?

JIM. Ohmigosh. Ya got a look at Betsy lately?

BEV (*eyes wide*). Oh, I *know*.

JIM. Give that girl a *wide berth*.

BEV. Jim, can I get you some iced tea?

RUSS (*to* BEV). Maybe call back and ask him to come later.

BEV. It was a payphone. (*To* JIM.) Oh oh oh oh oh! I know!
Now wait. Now Jim: I am going to ask you a question:

JIM. Huh-oh!

BEV (*to* RUSS). And don't help him. (*To* JIM.) Now: I want
you to tell Russ what you think the word *Neapolitan* means.

RUSS (*to* JIM). She thought –

BEV. *Shhhhhh!!!* You're not allowed to say.

JIM. Well, that'd be your basic vanilla, strawb –

BEV. No no. The *derivation*.

RUSS. I *told* her what I th –

BEV (*to* RUSS). *Shhhhh!!!*

JIM. Uh, think it's *Naples*, isn't it?

BEV. Ohhhhh, *phooey*.

JIM. Or *Napoli*, as we like to say.

   FRANCINE *enters*.

BEV. You two are *cheating*. And then – well, Russ's in a funny
mood… he keeps going – (*Trying to do what* RUSS *did*.)
Oo-lan Ba-tor!

JIM. Whatzat, capital of Nepal?

RUSS. Mongolia.

JIM. Mongolia. So then what's the *Nepalese* – Do ya say
Nepalese?

BEV (*chuckles, slaps* RUSS*'s arm*). I hope it's not Ne-*politan*!

RUSS. Kathmandu.

JIM. Kathmandu!

BEV. Oh, well, I don't even know why you two know these
things.

FRANCINE. Miz Stoller?

JIM. Knowledge is power, Bev.

BEV. Then I choose to remain *powerless*. (*To* RUSS.) Do it again.

RUSS. Do what?

BEV. How you said it.

RUSS. No.

BEV. *Do* it, Russ.

RUSS. No.

BEV. Do it for Jim.

RUSS. Bev?

BEV. Why *not*?

RUSS. Sorry, Jim.

BEV. Why for me but not for him?

RUSS. Well, for one thing, cuz it's not *funny*.

FRANCINE. Excuse me, I'm fixing to go, so if you need something else?

BEV. Oh. Yes. One thing. Francine, you remember that big trunk that's upstairs?

RUSS. No no no no. Bev?

BEV. She doesn't mind.

RUSS. Just told you I'm doing it.

BEV. You said it's a two-person job, and here's two of you right here.

RUSS. Well, what's the emergency?

JIM (*to* BEV). I *would* offer my services – (*Continues.*)

BEV (*overlapping*). Oh no no no no no.

JIM. – but I am under doctor's orders, believe it or not.

FRANCINE. Well, I'm just needing to leave by three thirty.

BEV (*resigned*). All right.

RUSS. Francine? *I* am going to move the gol-darned trunk.

FRANCINE. Yes, sir.

BEV (*to* JIM, *mock-privately*). That's what I get for trying.

FRANCINE *exits. Discomfort.*

JIM (*to* RUSS). Soooo –

BEV. Did you get any lunch, Jim? Do you want some – ?

JIM. No no no no no.

BEV. Since I guess we're *cleaning out the larder* and Russ seems to be eating every last thing in the icebox, so you'll have to fight him for the ice cream.

JIM. Not for me.

RUSS. Well, ya know. (*Shrugs.*) Can't pack ice cream in a suitcase.

BEV *finds this hilarious.*

BEV (*beside herself*). In a suitc – (*To* JIM.) *Did you hear what he just said?*

JIM (*chuckling as well*). Man's got a point!

BEV (*slaps* RUSS*'s shoulder*). *How do you think of those things?* Ice cream in a –

JIM. Not unless you're moving to the North Pole!

BEV *laughs harder.*

BEV. Thank goodness we're not moving *south*!

JIM. *That'd* be a mess. No question.

BEV *and* JIM *stop laughing, sigh. More discomfort, then:*

No question.

BEV. Well, I'm going to see what we *do* have.

BEV *exits into the kitchen, leaving* RUSS *and* JIM *alone. A beat, then:*

JIM. Whaddya, coming down with something?

RUSS. Who?

JIM. Bev said under the weather.

RUSS. Me?

JIM. And here ya sit in your PJs –

RUSS. No no no no no. I'm – Took the day to – Truck coming, so –

JIM. I gotcha.

RUSS. Coupla days off.

JIM. Playing hookey.

RUSS. No no.

JIM. Bev's your alibi.

RUSS. Just giving her a hand with stuff.

JIM. And you are hard at work, as I see.

RUSS (*smiles a little*). No. I just.

JIM. Kidding you.

RUSS. I know. I – I – Yup.

JIM. Woulda come to your aid there, only I'm dealing with a little, uh, issue.

RUSS. Oh yeah?

JIM. Piano I told ya about?

RUSS. Right?

JIM. Didja ever… (*Lowers voice.*) ever need a *truss*? Have to wear one of those?

RUSS. Uhhhh… Don't recall.

JIM. Oh, you'd recall it if you did.

RUSS. Guess not, then.

JIM. Then you are a *fortunate* man.

RUSS. I hear you.

JIM. Bend the knees or suffer the consequences.

RUSS. Yup.

Brief pause.

JIM. So, *Monday*, you said.

RUSS. Yup.

JIM. Off to the hinterlands.

RUSS. Monday it is.

BEV (*calling from off*). Jim, was that a yes or a no on the iced tea?

JIM (*calling back to her*). Uhhh, I would not say no to that.

BEV (*same*). Russ?

    RUSS *shakes his head*.

JIM (*same*). I believe Russ is declining your gracious offer.

BEV (*same*). I thought as much.

    Pause.

JIM. *Monday*.

RUSS. Indeed.

JIM. Head 'em up. Move 'em out.

RUSS. Yup.

JIM. And when ya start that Glen Meadows office?

RUSS. Monday after.

JIM. How about that.

RUSS. Yup.

JIM. And how's that shaping up?

RUSS. Oh, boy, now. That's a nice set-up.

JIM. I betcha.

RUSS. And *spacious*, that's the thing. And *carpeted*? And I got a look at that office they're putting me in. Tell you what I thought to myself, I thought what the heck do ya do with all this space? *Corner* office. Windows, two sides. But the space is the primary – That is just an… *extravagant* amount of space.

JIM. Elbow room.

RUSS. Other thing is, once we get situated up in the new place. The time it takes? Driveway to the parking lot? Know what that's gonna take me?

JIM. Five minutes.

RUSS. Six and a half.

JIM. Close enough.

RUSS. Timed it. Door to door.

JIM. Roll outta bed and *boom*.

RUSS. And Tom Perricone. I don't know if you know Tom. Colleague of mine. Now, he's going to relocate to that same office and they live right down here offa Larabee. You know what *that's* gonna take him on the expressway?

JIM. That's a drive.

RUSS. Thirty-five minutes. And that's no traffic.

JIM. Well, Judy and I are sure gonna miss having you two around.

RUSS. Well... Yeah.

Awkward pause.

JIM (*lowers voice, secretively*). And how's Bev doing?

RUSS. Oh, you know. Bev loves a project.

JIM. Keep her occupied.

RUSS. The *mind* occupied.

JIM. What, does she worry a lot?

RUSS. No. No more than –

JIM. About you?

RUSS. Me? No.

JIM. Ya seem good to me.

RUSS. I meant – you know how she gets.

JIM. Sure.

RUSS. Overexcited.

JIM. I can see that.

RUSS. Worked up over things. Minor things.

JIM. Things like?

RUSS. Oh, you know.

JIM. Not calling yourself a *minor thing*, are you?

RUSS (*beat, slightly irritated*). No, I didn't – I meant things like –

JIM (*chuckles*). Do *you* consider yourself a *minor thing*?

RUSS. Jim, I didn't – Well, actually, in the grand scheme of things I don't think any one of us is, uh… particularly – did Bev *ask* you to come over?

JIM. Nope.

RUSS. I mean, good to see you. Great to see you.

JIM. I mean, we *ran into* each other coupla days ago. Got to talking.

RUSS. Uh-huh.

JIM. Little about you. Since she cares about you.

RUSS. Right. Right.

Pause. RUSS *looks for* BEV.

The heck's she doing in there?

JIM. Everybody cares about you, Russ.

RUSS. Uh-huh. Uh-huh. Yup. Well. Tell ya what I think. And I'm not a psychiatrist or anything but I do think a lotta people today have this tendency, tendency to *brood* about stuff, which, if you ask me, is, is, is – well, short answer, it's *not productive*. And what *I'd* say to these people, were I to have a degree in psychiatry, I think my advice would be maybe, get up offa your rear end and *do* something.

JIM. Huh.

RUSS. Be my solution.

JIM. Uh-huh.

RUSS. Of course, what do I know?

JIM. I think you know plenty.

Pause. RUSS *turns*.

RUSS (*calling*). Hey, Bev?

JIM. Like, I think you know your son was a good man, no matter what. Hero to his country. Nothing changes that.

RUSS. Yup yup yup.

JIM. And I also think you know that sometimes talking about things that happen, painful things, maybe –

RUSS. Uh, you don't happen to have a degree in psychiatry *either*, do you, Jim?

JIM *stares*.

No? Just checking.

JIM. We all suffer, you know. Not like you and Bev, maybe, but –

RUSS. But, see, since what *I'm* doing here is, see, since I'm just minding *my own* business – (*Continues*.)

JIM (*overlapping*). But it doesn't hurt –

RUSS. – sorta seems to *me* you might save yourself the effort worrying about things you don't need to *concern* yourself with and furthermore – (*Continues*.)

JIM (*overlapping*). He's in a better place, Russ.

RUSS. – if you *do* keep going on about those things, Jim, well, I hate to have to put it this way, but what I think I might have to do is… uh… politely ask you to uh… (*Clears his throat*.) well, to go fuck yourself.

Pause.

JIM. Not sure there's a polite way to ask that.

RUSS *rises to exit*.

RUSS (*embarrassed*). Okay? So.

JIM. I just can't believe Kenneth would've wanted his own father to –

RUSS (*maintaining calm*). Yup. Yup. So, you can go fuck yourself, okay?

BEV *enters with* JIM*'s iced tea.*

BEV. So wait. So if it's *Napoli* in Italian, then wouldn't adding an E before the A just seem superfluous – (*Beat.*) What's happening?

JIM. Bev, I believe I will hit the road.

BEV. What are you – ? Russ?

RUSS. Going upstairs.

BEV. What happened?

JIM. Not to worry.

BEV (*to* RUSS). What did you do?

JIM. Another time.

BEV (*to* RUSS). Come back here.

JIM (*to* BEV). No no. Russ   BEV (*quietly to* RUSS). Why
made his feelings clear in –   are you being like this?
(*Continues.*)

JIM. – no uncertain terms.

RUSS (*to* BEV). Going up, now.

JIM. Terms maybe more appropriate for the *locker room* than the –

BEV (*to* JIM). I *told* you so. I *told* you what it's like. And he uses these ugly words in other people's presence – (*To* RUSS.) and I'm not some kind of *matron*, but what in the world is wrong with *civility*?

RUSS. Honey? I am not going to stand here with you and Jim and discuss – (*Continues.*)

BEV (*overlapping*). Well, you're being *ugly*, and I don't like *ugliness*.

RUSS. – *private* matters, matters that are between me and the memory of my son – (*Continues.*)

BEV (*to* JIM). I think his *mind* has been affected, I really do.

RUSS. – and if the two of you want to talk about Kenneth on your *own* time, if that gives you some kind of *comfort* –

BEV. And what's wrong with *comfort*? Are we not *allowed* any comfort any more?

RUSS. Well, Kenneth didn't get a whole lotta comfort, did he?

BEV. He was *sick*, Russ! And for you to use nasty words to Jim –

JIM. Nothing I haven't heard before.

RUSS (*moving upstairs*). Changing my shirt.

JIM. I was in the service, too, you know.

RUSS (*bitter laugh*). Oh right. And tell me again. How many people did *you* kill?

BEV. *Oh, for God's sake, stop it!!*

RUSS (*shouting*). Sat behind a *desk*, didn'tcha? Goddamn *coward*.

The doorbell rings. All stand in silence. BEV *covers her mouth. At the front door, we can see* ALBERT *peer through a small window.*

ALBERT (*from off*). Hello?

And still no one moves.

Anybody home?

JIM *crosses to open the door.*

JIM. Afternoon.

ALBERT (*to* JIM). Uh, how d'you do? I'm just here to –

BEV (*calling off*). Francine? Albert's here.

FRANCINE (*calling, from off*). Yes, ma'am. I'm coming.

BEV. She's on her way.

ALBERT. Thank you, ma'am.

JIM *does not know whether to invite* ALBERT *in or not. He turns to* BEV. RUSS *turns and exits up the stairs.* BEV *turns back to* ALBERT.

BEV. Albert, would you like to wait inside?

ALBERT. Uh. All right, thank you, ma'am.

BEV. I bet it's warm out there, isn't it?

ALBERT. Ohhh, yes it is.

BEV. Can I offer you some iced tea?

ALBERT. No. Thank you, though.

BEV. Well, I'm sure she'll be right along.

ALBERT. Thank you.

ALBERT *sits near the door, but within earshot of* JIM *and* BEV.

JIM (*whispering because of* ALBERT). I think maybe it's time for me –

BEV (*rapidly, whispering*). Oh please don't go, please don't, I just don't want to be alone with him right now. It makes me feel so alone – (*Continues.*)

JIM (*overlapping*). You're not alone.

BEV. – the way he sits up all night long. Last night he was just sitting there at three in the morning – (*Continues.*)

JIM (*overlapping*). I know. I do.

BEV. – and I say to him say don't you feel sleepy? Do you want to take a Sominex, or play some cards maybe, and he says *I don't see the point of it* as if there has to be some grand justification for every single thing that a person –

And now she notices ALBERT *rising and heading for the door.*

(*To* ALBERT.) – Wait. Yoo-hoo?

ALBERT (*having overheard*). S'all right.

BEV. Something wrong?

ALBERT. No no.

BEV. She said she's on her way.

ALBERT. I can wait outside.

BEV (*calling off*). *Francine*?

FRANCINE (*calling, from off*). *I'm coming*.

BEV. There she is.

> FRANCINE *enters in street clothes, with two large bags of hand-me-downs. She stops to put on her earrings.*

FRANCINE. I'm sorry. I guess I'm moving a little slower than usual.

BEV. And here's Albert waiting so patiently, if only I had *door-to-door service like Francine*!

FRANCINE. So, I'll see you Monday, then.

BEV. Albert, isn't this place just a *catastrophe*?

ALBERT. Oh, yes it is.

BEV (*to* ALBERT). I tell you, I don't know *what* I would do without a friend like Francine here, and on a *Saturday*, I mean she is just a treasure. What on earth are we going to do up there without her?

ALBERT. Well, I trust y'all can sort things out.

BEV (*to* FRANCINE). Oh, and maybe Monday we can see about that big trunk, why don't we?

FRANCINE. We'll make sure and do that.

BEV. I'd do it myself but I'm not a big strapping man like Albert here.

JIM. Afraid I've gotta exempt myself –

BEV. Oh no no no no no. Francine and I can manage.

ALBERT. What's it, a trunk, you said?

FRANCINE (*with a shake of the head to dissuade* ALBERT). A footlocker.

ALBERT. Where's it at?

BEV. No no no no no we just need to bring it down the stairs.

ALBERT. I don't mind.

BEV. Oh, thank you, but no.

FRANCINE (*to* BEV). But definitely Monday.

ALBERT. These stairs, here?

BEV. Oh no no no – I mean, it wouldn't take but two minutes.

FRANCINE (*to* BEV, *re: her bags*). It's just I got these things here to take care of.

ALBERT. I can put them in the car.

JIM. Oh, got yourself a car?

ALBERT. Yes, sir.

JIM (*looking out*). Whatzat, a Pontiac?

ALBERT. Yes, sir.

FRANCINE (*significantly, to* ALBERT). It's just that I'm afraid we're going to be late.

ALBERT (*not getting it*). Late for what?

FRANCINE. The place we gotta be?

ALBERT. The *place*?

FRANCINE. Remember?

ALBERT (*to* FRANCINE). The – What're you – ?

FRANCINE (*to* BEV). I'm sorry.

ALBERT (*to* FRANCINE). Said two minutes is all.

FRANCINE (*quiet, pointedly*). Well, I've got my *hands* full.

ALBERT. I just said I can put them in the –

FRANCINE (*testily, as they start to go*). *I* can put them in the car. *I* can do that.

BEV. Did you get the chafing dish?

FRANCINE. No, ma'am, thank you, though.

ALBERT (*to* BEV *and* JIM). Be right back.

ALBERT *opens the door to reveal* KARL, *about to ring the bell*.

KARL (*an oddly formal and uncomfortable-seeming man*). Ah. Unexpected. Uhhh…?

BEV. Hello, Karl.

KARL (*relieved*). Ah, Bev. *Voilà*.

ALBERT (*to* KARL, *squeezing past*). Excuse us, if you don't mind?

KARL (*to* ALBERT, *formally*). Not at all. After you, sir.

KARL *makes way for* ALBERT *and* FRANCINE *to pass*.

ALBERT (*to* FRANCINE, *as they exit, barely audible*). What is the *matter* with you?

KARL (*from the door, seeing* JIM). Ah. Jim, too. Hello, lad.

JIM. Karl.

BEV (*unenthusiastically*). Come on in, Karl.

KARL. Uhhh… (*As if working out a puzzle*.) Yes. Could do that. However, you'll recall, Bev, that Betsy currently happens to be, uh, how shall we say – ?

BEV. Ohhh, is it almost that time?

KARL. Uh, point *being*, that she did accompany me.

BEV. What do you – you mean she's in the *car*?

KARL. She is.

BEV. Well, for heaven's *sake*, Karl! Don't leave her out in a hot *car*.

KARL. Well, that was my thinking.

BEV. Bring her *in* with you.

KARL. Will do.

BEV. Of all *things*.

KARL (*as he goes*). Back in a flash.

As KARL *exits*, RUSS *descends the stairs in a clean shirt and shoes*. BEV *and* JIM *allow him to silently pass by them*.

He walks to the chair and collects the ice-cream carton. As
RUSS *is about to exit again:*

BEV. You changed your shirt.

RUSS *continues into the kitchen without responding. A*
moment, then:

JIM (*quietly*). Bev.

BEV (*whispering*). I know I'm being silly. I know I am, but –
(*Continues.*)

JIM (*overlapping*). Not at all. Not in the least.

BEV. – it's just that after two-and-a-half *years* you'd think that
with *time*, because that's supposed to be the thing that helps,
isn't it? A little bit of time – (*Continues.*)

JIM (*overlapping*). A great healer.

BEV. – and I thought with the new job and the move I thought
somehow he would start to let go of –

RUSS *returns from the kitchen.* BEV *goes silent. He goes to*
a door beneath the stairs, opens it, pulls a string to turn on a
light, and exits.

(*Calling after him.*) Where are you going, the basement?

RUSS (*calling, from off*). Yup.

BEV. Are you looking for something?

RUSS (*farther away*). Yup.

The front door opens. KARL *escorts his wife* BETSY, *who is*
eight months pregnant, and who also happens to be totally
deaf.

KARL. Here we are, then.

BEV. Oh, *there she is!*

BETSY. Hehhyoooh, Behhhh. [*Translation:* Hello, Bev.]

BEV (*over-enunciating for* BETSY's *benefit*). Well, just *look* at
you! My *goodness*. You are just the *biggest* thing.

BETSY. Ah nohhh! Eee toooor. Ah so beee!!! [I know! It's true.
I'm so big.]

KARL. Took the liberty of not ringing the bell.

BEV. Betsy, you know Jim.

JIM. Indeed she does.

BETSY. Hah Jeee. [Hi Jim.]

> JIM *shows off his sign-language skills to* BETSY, *finger-spelling the last word.*

BEV. Oh, well, now look at *that*. Look at them go. What is that about? Somebody translate!

BETSY (*laughing, to* KARL). Huhuhuuh!! *Kaaaaa!!*

JIM (*chuckling along*). Uh-oh! What did I do? Did I misspell?

> BETSY *signs to* KARL.

KARL (*chuckles*). Uh, it seems, Jim, that you, uh, told Betsy that she was expecting a *storm*!!

BEV. *No!* He meant stork! You meant *stork*, didn't you?

BETSY (*pantomimes umbrella*). Ahneemah-umbrayah! [I need my umbrella!]

> *All laugh.*

BEV. Her *umbrella*! (*To* BETSY.) I understood that!

KARL. Have to check the weather report!

BEV. A *storm*, I'm going to tell that to Russ.

JIM (*conceding his mistake*). Must have rusty fingers!!

> *All chuckle.*

BETSY (*to* KARL, *asking for translation*). Kaaaah?

KARL (*speaks as he signs*). Uh, Jim says *his fingers are rusty.*

> BETSY *laughs and covers her mouth.*

BEV. See? She understands.

BETSY (*to* JIM, *imitating washing hands*). Jeee, mehbbe yew neeee sooohh!! [Jim, maybe you need soap!]

BEV (*explaining to* JIM). *Soap*. For the rust on your –

JIM (*to* BEV). No, I understood.

More polite laughing.

RUSS *emerges from the basement, carrying a large shovel.*

KARL. And there's the man himself! Thought he'd absconded!

BEV (*to* RUSS). The Lindners are here.

BETSY. Hehhyoooo, Ruuuuhhh. [Hello, Russ.]

RUSS. Betsy. (*To* BEV.) Ya seen my gloves anywhere?

KARL (*re: the shovel*). Tunnelling to China, are we?

RUSS (*to* BEV). Pair of work gloves?

BEV (*to* KARL). Do you know I just got through saying how Russ and I never entertain and here it is a regular neighbourhood social!

KARL. Well, we shan't be long.

BEV. Karl, do you suppose Betsy would like a glass of iced tea?

KARL (BETSY *does not see him*). Bets –? (*To* BEV.) Point to me.

BEV (*to* BETSY, *over-enunciated*). *Betsy, look at Karl.*

BETSY *looks at* KARL.

KARL (*to* BETSY, *signing simultaneously*). *Bev wants to know if you want some iced tea to drink?*

BETSY. Ohhh, yehhhpeee. Dahhnyoo, Behhh. [Oh, yes please. Thank you, Bev.]

RUSS (*to* BEV). Know the gloves I'm talking about?

BEV. Well, Karl's here. I thought you were going to talk to Karl.

FRANCINE *and* ALBERT *have entered and started up the stairs.*

RUSS. The heck's going on?

BEV. Nothing. Now, we two girls are going to the refreshment stand, so you boys'll have to manage on your own.

KARL. Have no fear.

BEV (*while exiting*). *So how are you feeling, Betsy? Are you tired?*

BETSY. Noooo, ahhhh fiiieee, Behhhh, reeeee. [No, I'm fine, Bev, really.]

BETSY *and* BEV *exit to the kitchen.*

KARL. Now, Russ, Bev tells me you're indisposed, and normally I'd – (*Realises.*) Ah. Not *contagious*, is it?

RUSS. Is what?

KARL. Hate for Betsy to, uh, come into contact with any –

RUSS. Not contagious.

KARL. Can't be too careful. Or possibly one can. Anyway, hate to commandeer your Saturday afternoon here, *a man's home*, as they say, but, as we haven't seen your face at Rotary of late I thought I might – (*Continues.*)

RUSS (*overlapping*). What's on your mind, Karl?

KARL. – intrude upon the sanctity of – what'd you say?

RUSS. What's on your mind?

KARL. Ah. Well. Firstly – May I sit?

RUSS. Yeah, yeah.

JIM. Karl, I will be taking my leave.

KARL. Not on my account?

JIM. Parish business.

KARL. Uh, well, truth to tell, Jim, we might actually benefit from your insight here?

JIM (*looks at watch*). Uhhhhh –

KARL. If it's not pressing?

JIM. Actually –

KARL. Not to usurp your authority, Russ. Your castle. You are the king.

RUSS. What's on your mind?

KARL (*as he sits on a box*). Is this safe?

RUSS. Anywhere.

KARL. No breakables? And Jim?

JIM (*sits, looking at* RUSS). Uhh… minute or two.

KARL. Good. Good good good. So.

> BEV *opens the kitchen door.*

BEV. Iced tea for you, Karl?

KARL. Ah. Problem *being* that I *do* have some sensitivity to the cold beverages, so my question would be is the tea *chilled*, by which I mean has it been *in* the Frigidaire?

BEV (*enduring him*). No, Karl.

KARL. Then, if I might have a serving *minus* the ice? That would suit me fine.

BEV. All right, Karl.

> BEV *closes the door.*

KARL. Anyway, Russ, if you don't mind, I will proceed directly to, dare I say, *the crux*. So. First and foremost, as far as matters of *community* are concerned, I've always maintained –

> BEV *and* BETSY *enter from the kitchen with glasses of iced tea.*

BEV. All right, you boys.

KARL (*panicky about* BETSY). What's –? Is something – ?

BEV (*handing* KARL *his tea*). She's *fine*, Karl.

KARL. Is that tea she's drinking?

BEV. Yes, Karl.

KARL. Slow sips. Small sips.

BEV. All right, Karl.

BETSY and BEV *sit at the dining table, away from the men. They begin to communicate via pad and pencil.*

RUSS. You were saying?

KARL (*takes glasses off, mops brow*). Tad overwrought, I suppose. (*Lowers voice.*) What with Betsy's condition, but… well, given our history of two years ago, I don't know, Russ, if you knew the details of that.

RUSS. Some, yup.

KARL. And Jim: source of great comfort for us during all of that. (*Beat, then to* RUSS.) It was the umbilical cord. Nature of the problem.

RUSS. I knew that.

KARL. Wrapped around the… (*Indicates his neck.*) Exactly. So, no one at fault. No one to *blame*. But these tragedies do come along. As you and Bev well know.

JIM. What're you hoping? Boy or girl?

KARL. Ah, no. Touch wood. No tempting fate.

JIM. There you go.

KARL (*back to* RUSS). Not to compare *our* little… setback… to what the two of you endured, but –

RUSS. Something about a *crux*?

KARL. Right you are. Well: to backtrack. I take it, Russ, you're aware that the Community Association meets the first Tuesday of each month? And as I'm sure you know, Don Skinner is part of the steering committee. And somehow it came to Don's attention at this late juncture that Ted Driscoll had found a buyer for this house and I have to say it *did* come as something of a shock when Don told us what sort of people they were.

RUSS. What sort of people are they?

Pause. KARL *stares at* RUSS.

KARL. Well. (*Chuckles.*) Uhh… Huh. I suppose I'm forced to consider the possibility that you actually don't *know*.

RUSS. Don't know *what*?

KARL. Well, I mean. That they're coloured.

RUSS. Who are?

KARL. The family. It's a coloured family.

Pause.

So: I contacted the family –

JIM. Wait wait wait.

KARL (*to* RUSS). You're saying Ted never bothered to tell you?

RUSS. We, uhh… sort of gave Ted free rein on the –

JIM. I don't think you're right on this one, Karl.

KARL. Oh, but I am. Oh, I've spoken with the family.

RUSS. Bev?

JIM. On the *telephone?*

KARL. Oh, no. As a matter of fact, Betsy and I've just come directly from… (*Beat, for effect.*) Well, from *Hamilton Park*.

BEV (*to* RUSS). What is it?

RUSS. C'mere a second.

KARL. Now, Russ: you know as well as I do that this is a progressive community.

BEV (*to* RUSS *as she joins them*). What's he talking about?

KARL. If you take the case of Gelman's grocery: that's a fine example of how we've all embraced a different way of thinking –

RUSS. Slow down a second. Bev, get Ted Driscoll on the phone.

BEV (*to* RUSS). What for?

RUSS. Karl says. Karl is *claiming* –

KARL. Russ, I have met *personally* with the family, and –

BEV. What family?

RUSS. He claims this family. The family to whom Ted sold the house.

KARL. It's a coloured family.

Pause. JIM *shakes his head.*

JIM (*to* KARL). Sorry, don't we say *Negro*, now?

KARL (*irritated*). I *say* Negro – (*Continues.*)

JIM (*overlapping*). Well, it's only common courtesy, and I'm – (*Continues.*)

KARL. – I say them interchangeably – (*Continues.*)

JIM. – not trying to tell you how to conduct your business.

KARL. – and of course I said *Negro* to them – No, I think we both know what you're doing.

JIM. And furthermore, I don't think Ted would pull a stunt like that.

KARL. Yes. We all admire Ted. But I don't think any of us would accuse him of putting the community's interests ahead of his own.

BEV. Oh, this is ridiculous.

KARL. And I don't think any of us have forgotten what happened with the family that moved onto Kostner Avenue last year. Now, Kostner Avenue is *one* thing, but *Clybourne Street* –

BEV. Waitwaitwait. Karl, are you *sure*?

KARL. I was sitting with them not two hours ago.

BEV. But isn't it possible that they're… I don't know, *Mediterranean*, or – ?

KARL. Bev, they are *one hundred per cent*. And I don't know how much time any of you have spent in Hamilton Park, but Betsy was waiting in the car and I can tell you, there are some *unsavoury* characters.

RUSS. Karl?

KARL. But, in the case of Gelman's: I think there was some mistrust at first, having been Kopeckne's Market for such a long time, but in the end of all, Murray Gelman found a way to *fit* in.

BEV. And they hired the Wheeler boy.

JIM. Is he the one with the – ? (*Indicates his head*.)

BEV. He's the – you know. (*Does the same*.)

KARL. And *fitting into* a community is really what it all comes down to.

A very loud THUMP from upstairs.

RUSS. The heck is going *on* up there?

KARL. Now, some would say change is inevitable. And I can support that, if it's change for the better. But I'll tell you what I *can't* support, and that's disregarding the needs of the people who *live* in a community.

BEV. But don't they have needs, too?

KARL. Don't who?

BEV. The family.

KARL. Which family?

BEV. The ones who –

KARL. The *purchasers*?

BEV. I mean, in, in, in, in *principle*, don't we *all* deserve to – Shouldn't we *all* have the opportunity to, to, to –

KARL (*chuckles with amazement, shakes his head*). Well, *Bev*.

JIM. In *principle*, no question.

KARL. But you can't live in a *principle*, can you? Gotta live in a *house*.

BEV. And so do they.

KARL. Not in *this* house, they don't.

JIM. But here's the real question:

KARL. And what happened to *love thy neighbour*? If we're being so principled.

BEV. They would *become* our neighbours.

KARL. And what about the neighbours you already *have,* Bev?

BEV. I care about them, too!

KARL. Well, I'm afraid you can't have it both ways.

RUSS. Okay. Assuming –

BEV. Wait. Why not?

KARL. Well, do the boundaries of the neighbourhood extend indefinitely? Who shall we invite next, the *Red Chinese*?

ALBERT *has tentatively come to the bottom of the stairs, jacket off.*

JIM. But the key question is this:

BEV. No. Why *not* have it both ways?

KARL. Darling, I came to talk to Russ.

ALBERT. 'Scuse me, ma'am?

BEV. Why not, if it would *benefit* someone?

JIM. But *would* they benefit?

BEV. If we could make them our *neighbours*.

KARL. But they won't be *your* neighbours, Bev. *You're* the ones moving away!

JIM. The question is, and it's one worth asking:

ALBERT. Sorry to bother you?

RUSS (*taking charge*). Okay. Let's *assume* your information is correct.

Then suddenly, an enormous green Army footlocker comes sliding down the stairs with a noisy thumpeta-thumpeta-thumpeta-thump. ALBERT *jumps out of the way.*

ALBERT.	FRANCINE	BEV. Oh oh	RUSS. *Aw, for*
Sorry, sir,	(*top of the*	oh. What	*crying out*
my fault!	*stairs*).	happened?	*loud!* What
That was	*That was*	Is everyone	the heck is
me. That	*my fault!*	all right?	the matter
was all my	*I'm sorry!*		with
doing.			people?
			Bev, darn it
			all!!

BEV (*to* RUSS). Why are you shouting? Everything's *fine*, so – (*Continues*.)

RUSS. Well, what did I *tell* you? – (*Continues*.)

BEV. – please don't do that, they're just trying to *help* –

RUSS. – I *told* you I'd do it. You heard me plain as day.

BETSY. Eeeen *ahhhh* hurrrrhhh daaaaaa! [Even *I* heard that!]

KARL (*to* RUSS *and* BEV). Little *mishap*, is it?

ALBERT. Little trouble making the corner, is all.

FRANCINE (*now downstairs*). I'm sorry. It's heavy and I lost my gr –

RUSS (*to* ALBERT). Just leave the darn thing where it is.

BEV. We can't leave it there.

KARL. May one be of assistance?

JIM. Lend you a hand if I could, but –

ALBERT. What should we – ? Would you prefer it if I – ?

RUSS (*to* ALBERT). Just, just, just, just *leave* it.

BEV. But it's blocking the way.

FRANCINE. No, ma'am, I can step over –

ALBERT. It's all right. I got her.

> ALBERT *helps* FRANCINE *climb over the box that now blocks the stairs*.

KARL. Anyway, let's not drag this out *ad infinitum*.

> RUSS, *fed up, rises and exits to the basement, slamming the door behind him*.

BEV. Russ, *don't*.

JIM (*to* KARL). One second, if I might? (*To* FRANCINE.) Sorry. Uh, *Francine*, is it?

FRANCINE. Yes, sir?

JIM. Francine, we've just been having a little conversation here, and I was wondering if maybe you could spare us a couple of minutes of your time?

KARL. What good does that do? Go next door. Talk to the Olsens. Talk to those who stand to lose.

JIM (*ignoring him, to* FRANCINE). I want to pose a little hypothetical to you. What if we said this: let's imagine you and your husband here, let's say that the two of you had the opportunity to move from your current home into a different neighbourhood, and let's say that neighbourhood happened to be this one.

FRANCINE. Well, I don't think that we would, financially –

JIM. But for the sake of argument. Say you had the wherewithal. Would this be the sort of neighbourhood you'd find an attractive place in which to live?

FRANCINE *hesitates*.

BEV. Oh, this is so sil –

FRANCINE. It's a very nice neighbourhood.

JIM (*to* FRANCINE). No, I'm asking, would the two of you – Would your fam – I assume you have children?

FRANCINE. Three children.

JIM. Oh, super. So, with your children, might this be the sort of place, bearing in mind that they, too, would stand to be affected – ?

BEV. This is confusing things! It's confusing the issue!

FRANCINE (*to* JIM). It's a very lovely neighbourh –

JIM. No, be honest. We want you to say.

BEV (*to* FRANCINE). I think what Jim is asking, in his way –

ALBERT. He means living next to white folks.

BEV. I – I – I – I – well, yes.

Pause.

FRANCINE. Well –

BEV. Francine and I have, over the years, the *two of us* have shared so many wonderful – (*To* FRANCINE.) Remember that time the *squirrel* came through the window?

FRANCINE (*smiling, indulging* BEV). Yes I do.

BEV. That was just the silliest – the two of us were just *hysterical*, weren't we?

KARL (*pressing ahead, to* FRANCINE). Think of it this way.

BEV (*to the others*). We still laugh about that.

KARL. I think that you'd agree, I'm assuming, that in the world, there exist certain *differences*. Agreed?

FRANCINE. What sort of differences?

KARL. That people *live* differently.

FRANCINE (*unsure*)…. Yes?

KARL. From one another.

FRANCINE. I agree with that.

KARL. Different customs, different… well, different *foods*, even. And those diff – here's a funny – my wife Betsy, now, Betsy's family happens to be Scandinavian, and on holidays they eat a thing known as *lutefisk*. And this is a dish, which I can tell you… (*He chuckles.*) is *not* to my liking *at all*. It's… *oh* my goodness, let's just say it's gelatinous.

BEV (*indicating for him to stop*). Karl?

BETSY (*to* BEV). Whaaaaa sehhhhh? [What did he say?]

BEV (*over-enunciating*). *Lutefisk*.

BETSY. Whaaaaaa ?

BEV. *Lutefi* – Karl, can you tell her?

KARL (*holds up a finger to* BETSY). In a moment.

BEV (*taking up her pad*). I'll write it down.

KARL (*to* FRANCINE). So, certain groups, they tend to *eat* certain things, am I right?

FRANCINE. I've never had that dish.

KARL. But, for example, if Mrs Stoller here were to send you to shop at Gelman's. Do you find, when you're standing in the aisles *at* Gelman's, does it generally strike you as the kind of market where you could find the particular foods *your* family enjoys?

FRANCINE. It's a *very* nice store.

JIM (*interposing*). What if we were to say *this*:

FRANCINE. Mr Gelman's a nice man.

> BEV *hands* BETSY *the pad of paper.*

KARL. But, I mean, your *preferred* food items, would such things even be *available* at Gelman's?

ALBERT. Do they *carry* collards and pig feet?

> FRANCINE *shoots a look at* ALBERT.

Cuz I sho couldn't shop nowhere didn' sell no pig feet.

> *Pause. All stare at* ALBERT.

JIM. Well, I think Albert's being *humorous* here, but –

BETSY (*having deciphered* BEV*'s handwriting*). Ohhhh, *loo-feee*! [Lutefisk]. (*To* BEV.) Ah *lye* loofee! [I *like* lutefisk.]

JIM. But I will say this –

FRANCINE (*to* KARL). I like spaghetti and meatballs.

> KARL *quiets* BETSY.

JIM. – you do find differences in modes of *worship*. If you take First Presbyterian. Now, that's a church down in Hamilton Park and I've taken fellowship there and I can tell you, the differences are notable.

BEV. Jim?

JIM. Not a *value* judgment. Apples and oranges. Just as how we have our organ here at St Thomas, for accompaniment, whereas at First Presbyterian, they prefer a piano and, occasionally... (*Chuckles.*) well, *tambourines*.

BEV. What's wrong with tambourines?

JIM. Nothing *wrong*.

BEV. I *like* tambourines.

JIM. I like tambourines as much as the next person.

> RUSS *returns from the basement carrying his work gloves.*
> *He is calmer.*

KARL. Well, let me ask this. (*To* BEV.) Excuse me. (*To*
FRANCINE.) Francine, was it?

FRANCINE. Yessir.

KARL. Francine, may I ask? Do you *ski*?

FRANCINE. Do I – ?

KARL. Or your husband? Either of you?

FRANCINE. Ski?

KARL. Downhill skiing?

FRANCINE. We don't ski, no.

KARL. And this is my point. The children who attend St
Stanislaus. Once a year we take the middle-schoolers up to
Indianhead Mountain, and I can tell you, in all the time I've
been there, I have not *once* seen a coloured family on those
slopes. Now, what accounts for that? Certainly not any
deficit in ability, so what I have to conclude is that, for some
reason, there is just something about the pastime of skiing
that doesn't appeal to the Negro community. And feel free to
prove me wrong.

RUSS. Karl.

KARL. But you'll have to show me where to find the skiing
Negroes!

RUSS. *Karl!*

BEV. Can we all modulate our voices?

RUSS. It's sold, Karl. The house is sold.

KARL. I understand that.

RUSS. The ink is dry.

KARL. And we all understand your reasons and no one holds that against you.

RUSS. Truck's coming on Monday.

KARL. Fully aware.

RUSS. And that's all there is to that.

KARL. *However*. (*Beat*.) There is *one* possibility.

RUSS. Nope. Nope.

KARL. If you'll hear me out.

RUSS. Don't see the point.

KARL. Because we went ahead and made a counter-offer to these people.

BEV. Who did?

KARL. The Community Association.

BEV. An offer on *this* house?

KARL. Very reasonable offer.

BEV (*baffled*). But, but, but, they just *bought* it, Karl!

KARL. As opposed to the amount for which *you* offered the property, Russ, which was *far* below the assessor's value – (*Continues*.)

RUSS (*overlapping*). Well, we're entitled to *give* it away if that's our prerogative.

KARL. – for this type of residence, all of which is neither here nor there, since the family *rejected* our offer. However:

BEV (*to* RUSS). Why are we even *talking* about this?

KARL. Don has pointed out to me, that, as the seller of the property, you do have a sixty-day option to place it in receivership with the transacting bank to indemnify yourself against liability. Now, that's generally with commercial properties, but in this instance – (*Continues*.)

RUSS (*slowly, overlapping*). Nope. Nope. Nope. Nope. Nope.

KARL. – I think that, inasmuch as Ted *deceived* you about the buyers, that the bank *could* still halt the sale and it would be a simple – (*Continues.*)

RUSS (*overlapping*). Karl?

KARL. – matter of a signature, if I could finish?

RUSS. Prefer it if you didn't.

BETSY. Kaahhhh?

BEV. And for all we know, this family could be perfectly lovely.

KARL. Well, that's hardly the point, is it?

BEV. Maybe it's a point to consider.

KARL (*with a chuckle*). Bev, I'm not here to solve society's problems. I'm simply telling you what will happen, and it will happen as follows: first one family will leave, then another, and another, and each time they do, the values of these properties will decline, and once that process begins, once you break that egg, Bev, all the king's horses, etcetera – (*Continues.*)

BETSY (*overlapping*). Kaahhh?

KARL. – and *some* of us, you see, those who *don't* have the opportunity to simply pick up and move at the drop of a hat, then *those* folks are left holding the bag, and it's a fairly *worthless* bag, at that point.

BEV. I don't like the tone this is taking.

RUSS (*to* KARL). Okay. Tell you what.

KARL. And let's imagine if the tables were turned. (*Re: FRANCINE and* ALBERT.) Suppose a number of *white* families started marching into *their* commun – ? Well, actually, that might be to their *advantage*, but – (*Continues.*)

RUSS. *Karl.*

KARL. – you do see my point.

RUSS. Need you to stop now.

KARL. Sorry. (*Beat.*) Maybe not handled with the – (*Continues.*)

RUSS. It's all right.

KARL. – utmost delicacy.

RUSS. But maybe time to let it drop.

KARL. Didn't mean to turn it into a public referendum. (*Beat.*) But you do understand –

RUSS. No no no no no. That's it. You hear me? Done. All done.

Pause. In the near distance a church bell begins to ring.

JIM (*quietly looking at his watch*). Is it four o'clock?

KARL. Well, Russ, if I might –

RUSS. Nope. Nope.

KARL. If I could just say this:

RUSS. No. Karl?

KARL. Well, if you'd let me –

RUSS. No. No more.

KARL. Uhhh… (*Chuckling.*) *Bev?* I get the impression your husband is telling me I'm not permitted to *speak*.

RUSS. Don't think it's a good idea.

KARL. Well, Russ, I'm going to ask you at least to keep an open – ?

RUSS. *Karl!* What'd I just ask you?

KARL. Well, I think you're being a tad unreasonable.

RUSS. Well, *I* think we've reached the end of this particular discussion.

KARL. Is that right?

RUSS. Afraid it is.

KARL. Just like that.

RUSS. Just like that.

Another pause.

KARL. Then what about this:

RUSS. *Karl!?*

KARL. Well, I believe the Constitution endows me with a *right* to speak.

RUSS. Well, then you can go and do that in your own home.

KARL. Bev…? (*Laughs.*) He's not being serious, is he?

RUSS. Karl?

KARL (*laughs*). Am I being *silenced*?

RUSS. Not going to ask you again.

KARL. Well, this is a new experience for me.

RUSS. So be it.

KARL. Bit like the Soviet Union. (*Laughs.*) I am truly surprised.

RUSS. Well, *surprise*.

KARL. And a little disappointed.

RUSS. Sorry to disappoint you.

KARL (*shakes his head*). A real shame. For all concerned.

RUSS. Well, that's the way things go sometimes.

KARL. Apparently so.

RUSS. Anyway. Appreciate you stopping by.

KARL. I see.

RUSS. Betsy, too.

KARL. Very well.

BETSY. Kaaaaahhhh?

RUSS. Okay then? Okay.

Silence. KARL *stands and moves toward* BETSY. *They slowly exit through the open door.*

BETSY (*quietly as they exit*). Kaahhh, whaah happaaahh?

FRANCINE. Miz Stoller, if we're done talking here?

JIM (*rising*). Yes, you know, I think *I* will take this opportunity –

But KARL *immediately returns,* BETSY *following.*

KARL. However:

JIM (*quietly*). Karl, don't.

KARL (*very slowly, carefully*). I *don't* imagine that… this particular family are *entirely* aware of *why* they've found such an agreeable price for the property. Don't suppose they know *that* aspect of it, do they? And let's say someone was to inform them of those facts. Let's say *that* was to happen.

RUSS (*chuckles dangerously*). Really don't know when to quit, do ya?

KARL. Because I think that might be an interesting conversation to have.

FRANCINE (*beat, then to* BEV). So I'll be seeing you on Mon –

RUSS (*maintaining control*). Well, Karl? You go ahead and do what you think is right, but I'll tell you one thing: what you're going to do right *now* is – (*Continues.*)

KARL (*overlapping*). Well, I have a responsibility to the community as a whole. I can't afford to – (*Continues.*)

RUSS. – you're going to take yourself right through that door and out of this house.

KARL (*overlapping*). – simply pursue my own selfish interests.

RUSS (*maintaining calm*). Man, what a son of a bitch.

BEV. Russ, don't.

RUSS (*to* KARL). If you honestly think I give a rat's ass about the goddamn – (*Continues.*)

JIM (*overlapping*). Okay. Okay.

RUSS. – what, ya mean the *community* where every time I go for a haircut, where they all sit and stare like the goddamn

Grim Reaper walked in the barber-shop door? *That* community? (*Continues*.)

KARL (*overlapping*). My wife is two weeks away from giving birth to a *child*.

RUSS. Where, Bev stops at Gelman's for a quart of milk and they look at her like she's got the goddamn plague? That the community I'm supposed to be looking out for?

KARL. A community with *soon-to-be children*.

JIM. The Apostle Matthew –

RUSS (*to* JIM). Oh no no no. *I'm* talking now.

BEV (*to* FRANCINE *and* ALBERT). I am ashamed of every one of us.

BETSY (*tugging at* KARL's *sleeve*). Kaaaaaah?

KARL. Betsy, wait in the car.

RUSS. Well, you go right ahead and you tell those folks whatever you want, Karl. And while you're at it why don't you tell 'em about everything *the community* did for my son. I mean *Jesus Christ*, Murray Gelman even goes and hires a goddamn *retarded* kid, but *my* boy? Sorry. No work for you, bub.

JIM. People were frightened, Russ.

RUSS (*contemptuous*). Ahh, of *what?* He was gonna *snap*? Gonna go and kill another bunch of people? Send him off to defend the goddamn country, he does like he's *told* only to find out the kinda sons of bitches he's defending?

BEV (*forthright*). He did not do the things they claimed he did. He would never –

RUSS. *Ah, Jesus, of course he did, Bev! He confessed to what he did!* Sit around all day with your head in the sand, it doesn't change the facts of what he *did*.

BEV. Not to innocent people in that country. And not to women or children. I mean, maybe he lost his temper in a –

RUSS. *Ah, for Christ's sake. What do you think happens in a goddamn war? They told him to secure the territory,* not go knocking on doors asking *permission*. And if he was man enough to admit what he did, maybe you oughta have the decency to do the same damn thing.

BEV (*turning to* FRANCINE *for support*). You remember. Francine remembers what he was like.

RUSS *makes a sound of disgust and goes to the footlocker. Under the following, he unlocks and opens the lid.*

How he loved to read and think. That's just the kind of boy he was, wasn't it?

FRANCINE. Yes, ma'am.

BEV (*to* FRANCINE). And the drawings? The most realistic drawings. I think a lot of people didn't realise –

KARL. Bev, it was never my intention to stir up – (*Continues.*)

BEV (*overlapping*). Ohhh, no, I think maybe it was.

KARL. – such acrimonious feelings, but there is a situation, which –

BEV. Well, maybe if you had known my son a little better. If anyone had taken the time, the way that Francine took the time –

RUSS *has produced an envelope from the footlocker. He steps forward, removing the letter – on yellow legal paper.*

RUSS. Here you go, Karl. Let's all read a little something, shall we?

BEV. What are you – ?

RUSS (*reading*). *Dear Mom and Dad.*

BEV (*realising*). *Stop it!!!*

RUSS (*reading*). *I know you'll probably blame yourselves –*

BEV (*standing, losing it completely*). Russ, stop it stop it stop stop stop it!!!!

JIM. Russ. Don't.   KARL (*to* RUSS). I think you're unstable, Russ. I really do.

BEV (*turning back to* JIM). *You see what this is like? You see?* (*To* RUSS.) *Well, I refuse to live this way any longer!!*

She goes into the bathroom and slams the door behind her.

RUSS (*starting over, calmly*). *Dear Mom and Dad.*

JIM. Russ?

RUSS. *I know you'll probably blame yourselves for what I've done –*

JIM. Need you to calm down.

RUSS. And *you* can go fuck yourself.

KARL. Well, *that* is over the line, mister. That is not language I will tolerate in front of my wife.

Beat. Then:

RUSS. She's *deaf*, Karl!! Completely – (*Waving to* BETSY, *fake-jolly*.) Hello, Betsy! Go fuck yourself!

BETSY *smiles, waves back.*

So here's what I'll do for you, Karl: make ya ten copies of this, you can hand 'em out at Rotary. Or better yet. Put it in the newsletter. Rotary News: Kid comes back from Korea, goes upstairs and wraps an extension cord around his neck. Talk that over at the lunch buffet next week.

BETSY (*barely audible*). Kaahhh?

RUSS. And Francine walking in at nine in the morning to find him there. You be my guest, Karl. You go ahead and tell those people what kind of house they're moving into and see if *that* stops 'em, because I'll tell you what, I don't give a shit if a hundred Ubangi tribesman with a bone through the nose overrun this goddamn place, cuz I'm *through with all of you,* ya motherfucking sons of bitches. Every one of you.

All stand in silence. We can hear BEV *crying from behind the bathroom door.* RUSS *slowly folds the letter. Finally:*

JIM. Maybe we should bow our heads for a second.

RUSS (*advancing on him*). Well, maybe I should punch you in the face.

RUSS *moves toward* JIM, *who, in backing away, inadvertently tumbles backwards over a box, toppling a floor lamp as he goes.*

ALBERT.	KARL. Easy	BETSY.	FRANCINE.
Whoa	now. Easy	Kaahh!!	What in
whoa whoa	does it…	Waaahhhh	God's
whoa	Careful –	happnee!?	name is
whoa!!	Betsy, go!		wrong with
	Betsy?		alla you
			people?

FRANCINE (*to* ALBERT). Stay out of it. Just stay out –

BETSY *runs out of the front door.* ALBERT *puts his hand on* RUSS's *shoulder.*

ALBERT. Hang on. Let's be civilised, now.

RUSS (*whirling on* ALBERT). Ohoho, don't you touch *me*.

ALBERT. Whoa whoa whoa.

RUSS. Putting your hands on *me*? No, *sir*. Not in *my* house you don't.

JIM (*gritting his teeth as he copes with his hernia*). I'm all right.

FRANCINE (*to* ALBERT). What the hell d'you think *you're* doing?

ALBERT. Who're you talking to?

FRANCINE. Who do you *think*?

KARL (*to* RUSS, *as he helps* JIM *to his feet*). Very manly, Russ. Threatening a *minister*.

ALBERT (*to* FRANCINE). Why're you talking to me like th –?

KARL (*to* RUSS). Very *masculine*.

FRANCINE. I think they're *all* a buncha idiots. And who's the biggest idiot of all to let yourself get dragged into the middle of it? Whatcha gonna be now, the big *peacemaker* come to save the day?

KARL *and* JIM *exit out the front door.*

KARL (*as he exits*). You're mentally unstable, Russ!

FRANCINE (*as she collects her bags*). Let 'em knock each other's *brains* out, for all *I* care. I'm done working for these people two days from now, and you never worked for 'em at *all*, so what the hell do you care *what* they do? And now I am going to the goddamn car.

FRANCINE *exits. During their marital squabble,* RUSS *has returned the letter to the footlocker and slammed the lid. He now drags it out of the room and into the kitchen.* ALBERT *is left alone in the middle of the room. He stands idly for a moment, then moves to right the overturned floor lamp. As he does,* BEV *enters from the bathroom, blowing her nose.*

ALBERT (*seeing* BEV). It's all right. Nothing broken.

BEV (*trying to be composed*). Oh oh oh don't mind that. But thank you so much.

ALBERT. No trouble.

BEV. And do let me offer you some money for your help.

ALBERT. Oh no, ma'am, that's all right.

BEV. Ohhh, are you sure?

ALBERT. Yes, ma'am.

BEV (*finding her purse*). Well, here, then. Let me at least give you fifty cents.

ALBERT. No, now you keep your money.

BEV. Or, how about a dollar? Take a dollar. I don't care.

ALBERT. Ma'am?

BEV. Or take two. It's just money.

ALBERT. Happy to help.

BEV. Or take something. You have to take something.

ALBERT. No, ma'am. But –

BEV. What about this chafing dish? Did you see this dish?

ALBERT. Well, we got plenty of dish –

BEV. Not one of these. Francine told me. (*Continues*.)

ALBERT (*overlapping*). Well, that's very kind of you, but –

BEV. She said you didn't have one and somebody should take it and – (*Continues*.)

ALBERT (*overlapping*). But we don't *need* it, ma'am.

BEV. – make use of it, so if you let me just wrap it for you.

ALBERT. *Ma'am, we don't want your things. Please. We got our own things.*

Pause. BEV *is shocked.*

BEV. *Well.*

ALBERT (*gently*). Trying to *explain* to you.

BEV. Well, if *that's* the attitude, then I just don't know what to say any more. I really don't. If that's what we're coming to.

ALBERT. Ma'am, everybody's sorry for your loss.

BEV (*holding back tears, nobly righteous*). You know, I would be… so *proud*. So *honoured* to have you and Francine as our neighbours. *And* the two children.

ALBERT. Three children.

BEV. Three chil – We would… Maybe we should *learn* what the other person eats. Maybe that would be the solution to some of the – If someday we could all sit down together, at one big table and, and, and, and… (*Trails into a whisper, shakes her head*.)

ALBERT. Evening, ma'am.

ALBERT *goes.* BEV *is left alone. After a moment,* RUSS *enters to fetch the shovel. He carries a pair of work gloves. Seeing* BEV, *he stops, unsure of what to say.*

BEV. Where'd you find the gloves?

RUSS. Under the sink.

BEV. And where are you going to dig the hole?

RUSS. Under the, uh… What's that big tree called?

BEV. The crepe myrtle.

RUSS. Under that.

BEV. Kind of late now, isn't it?

RUSS (*shrugs, light-hearted*). Do it tomorrow.

He leans the shovel against the wall. Pause. He stands idly, apologetically.

Kinda lost my temper.

BEV (*nods, then*). Well, that's what happens. As we know.

He slowly moves to sit in the chair he sat in at the start of the act, then looks back at BEV.

RUSS. Know what I did the other day? Up there at the house?

BEV. What?

RUSS. Driveway to the office. Timed it. Know how long that's gonna take me now?

BEV. Five minutes?

RUSS. Six and a half.

BEV. Well, you'll have a leisurely breakfast.

RUSS. Read the paper. Cup of coffee and *bang*.

BEV. Hmm.

RUSS. Five-oh-seven, right back at your doorstep.

BEV. And what'll I do in between?

RUSS is caught off-guard.

RUSS. I, I, uhhh… Well, gee, I guess, whatever you… Any number of…

BEV. Things.

RUSS. Projects.

BEV. Projects.

RUSS. To keep ya occupied.

BEV. I suppose you're right.

He turns on the transistor radio. Music. He looks back at BEV, *who stares into space.*

RUSS (*feebly, with a little sweep of the arm*). Ulan Bator!

BEV *smiles vaguely. The lights slowly fade.*

End of Act One.

ACT TWO

*September, 2009. Three o'clock, Saturday afternoon. There is
an overall shabbiness to the place that was not the case fifty
years earlier. The wooden staircase railing has been replaced
with a cheaper metal one. The oak mantelpiece and most of the
woodwork have been painted over several times, the fireplace
opening is bricked in, linoleum covers large areas of the
wooden floor and plaster has crumbled from the lath in places.
The kitchen door is now missing, and we can see through to an
exterior door. The front door stands propped open.*

*Lights rise to find six people facing each other in a rough circle.
To one side, STEVE and LINDSEY with KATHY, and to the
other KEVIN and LENA with TOM, all dressed in generic
casual clothes for a weekend afternoon. It is warm, and some
have iced drinks. LINDSEY is visibly pregnant. They sit upon
improvised seating – crates, abandoned furniture, etc. STEVE,
LINDSEY and KATHY study photocopied documents while the
others watch. Finally:*

TOM. Everybody good?

LINDSEY. I'm good.

STEVE. Good by me.

KATHY. Go for it.

TOM. So, I guess we should start right at the top.

STEVE. Question?

TOM. And I know we all got questions.

STEVE. The terminology?

TOM. So let's go one at a time: Steve.

STEVE. The term *frontage*?

TOM. Right.

STEVE. *Frontage* means?

LINDSEY. Where are we looking?

STEVE. First page.

TOM. *Frontage* means – (*Deferring to* KATHY.) Did you want
    to – ?

KATHY (*to* STEVE). Means the portion facing the street.

TOM. Thus, *front*.

STEVE (*to* TOM). Portion of the *property*?

KATHY (*to* STEVE). Of the structure.

STEVE (*to* TOM). Or portion of the *structure*?

TOM. The *facade*.

LINDSEY (*to* STEVE). I'm not seeing it.

KATHY (*to* LINDSEY). Second paragraph.

TOM (*to* LINDSEY). Bottom of the page.

STEVE (*to* LINDSEY). Where it says minimum recess of
    frontage?

TOM. Meaning, distance *from*.

KATHY (*to* TOM). From the edge of the *property*.

TOM. Exactly.

STEVE. Is what?

TOM. Is the recess.

STEVE. Not the *frontage*.

TOM (*to* STEVE). The frontage is what you're measuring to.

LINDSEY. Got it.

STEVE. I'm confused.

LINDSEY. And edge of the property means as measured from
    the *curb*?

KATHY. Correct.

TOM. Not from the *sidewalk*?

KATHY. From the curb.

TOM. Uhh – I'll check, but I don't think that's right.

KATHY. Up to and including.

TOM. But the sidewalk falls under the easement.

KATHY. Right?

TOM. So if it's part of the easement then it can't be part of the property, *per se*.

KATHY (*shaking her head*). By definition, the property is inclusive of the easement. The easement is legal passage *across* the property.

TOM. I don't think you're right.

KATHY. So, my understanding has always been –

KEVIN. Sorry, but – Does any of that really *matter*?

STEVE. It might.

KEVIN. I mean, I don't see how any of that really – (*Continues*.)

STEVE (*overlapping*). The language?

KEVIN. – impacts the outcome of the specific problem that –

STEVE. But *I* don't want to get in a situation where we *thought* we found a solution only to have it turn out we're screwed because of the *language*.

TOM. Wait.

LINDSEY (*to* STEVE). The language is clear to *me*.

TOM (*easily*). And who's being *screwed*?

STEVE. No no no.

TOM. No one's *screwing* any –

STEVE (*with a laugh*). I didn't mean like *screwed over*, I meant like maybe we *screwed ourselves*.

KEVIN. But how does that address the *height* issue?

TOM. The elevation.

STEVE (*to* TOM). But if the elevation is *conditional* on the perimeter, right?

TOM. That's the idea.

STEVE. If I'm reading correctly?

LINDSEY. But the perimeter isn't changing.

STEVE. But we're saying if it *could*.

LINDSEY. But we've established that it can't.

STEVE. But let's say it *did*.

LINDSEY. But I'm saying it won't.

STEVE. But I'm saying *what if*?

LINDSEY. But I'm saying *what did we discuss*?

KATHY*'s cellphone rings.*

STEVE (*to* LINDSEY, *with an easy laugh*). Okay, but do you have to *say* it like that?

LINDSEY. Like what?

STEVE. In that *way*?

LINDSEY. What *way*?

KATHY (*looking at the screen*). It's Hector. I'd better –

STEVE (*apologising to* KEVIN *and* LENA *for* LINDSEY). Sorry.

LINDSEY (*to* KEVIN *and* LENA). Did I say something in a *way*?

LENA. Not that I noticed.

KATHY (*answering phone*). Hi, Hector.

STEVE (*explaining to* KEVIN *and* LENA). The architect.

LINDSEY. Who really oughta be here.

KATHY (*on phone*). No, we're doing it now. No, we're here at the house.

KEVIN (*to* LINDSEY). Well, if you'd rather wait and do this when he *can* be?

STEVE. No no no.

LINDSEY (*to* STEVE). Well, I think we both know what's going to happen. (*Continues.*)

LINDSEY. He's going to go completely ballist – I'm just telling you what to expect.	STEVE. I don't give a – And, I believe he's working for *us*, right? Not the other way around.

KATHY (*on phone*). No, we're here with – (*To* TOM.) Tom, I forgot your last name.

TOM. Driscoll.

KATHY (*on phone*). Driscoll. So, Tom Driscoll and the people from the neighbourhood thing. Property-owners'… thing.

LINDSEY (*to* STEVE *and* LENA). And can I just say? I am in *love* with this neighbourhood.

KEVIN. Great neighbourhood.

LINDSEY. *Totally* great.

KATHY (*on phone*). Well, that's what we're trying to prevent.

LINDSEY. And the thing for me is? My current commute? Which is slowly eroding my soul?

KEVIN (*to* LINDSEY). How far ya coming from?

LINDSEY (*pointedly*). *Glen Meadow?*

KEVIN (*wincing*). Ooof.

LINDSEY. Exactly. And if you work downtown?

KEVIN. Where downtown?

LINDSEY (*'do you know it?'*). Donnelly & Faber?

KEVIN. On Jackson, right? Donnelly & – ?

LINDSEY. Yeah, Jackson, east of –

KEVIN. Yeah, I'm across the street.

LINDSEY. Where?

KEVIN. You know the big red building?

LINDSEY. I eat lunch in that building.

KEVIN. Capital Equities?

STEVE. You're kidding me.

KEVIN. I kid you not.

LINDSEY (*to* KEVIN). And from here to downtown is like, what, five minutes?

STEVE (*to* KEVIN). Ya ever meet Kyle Hendrickson?

KEVIN. I *work* with Kyle Hendrickson.

KATHY (*on phone*). No, but I do think you're being a *little* paranoid, because we're not going to let that happen.

LINDSEY (*to* KATHY). Lemme talk to him.

KATHY (*on phone*). *I'm* not going to let it happen.

LINDSEY. Kathy.

KATHY (*on phone*). Wait. Lindsey wants to –

LINDSEY. Lemme do it. (*Taking phone.*) Hector?

KATHY (*rolling her eyes*). I'm obviously not equipped to deal with –

LINDSEY (*on phone*). I thought you were in Seattle.

STEVE (*to* KATHY). What's the problem?

KATHY. Tell you later.

LINDSEY (*on phone, soothing*). No no no no. Kathy's here. Kathy's not going to let that –

LINDSEY *rolls her eyes at the others.*

STEVE (*to the others*). *Spaniards.*

LINDSEY (*whispering to the others*). Two seconds.

> LINDSEY *exits out the front door. Pause. The others wait.*

KEVIN (*to* STEVE). Spaniards?

STEVE. Architect, ya know.

KEVIN. Spanish.

STEVE. Temperamental.

KEVIN. Toro toro.

STEVE. Exactly.

TOM. Seemed cool to me.

STEVE. You talked to him?

TOM. On the phone, yeah.

STEVE. He's a good guy.

> *Little pause. Then, small talk.*

KATHY. We were in Spain last year.

KEVIN. S'that right?

KATHY. Me, my husband. Spain, Morocco.

STEVE (*explaining to* KEVIN). I just meant – with all the paperwork and everything? And then we add *him* into the mix?

KEVIN. I hear you.

STEVE. Cooler heads, ya know.

KEVIN. Prevail.

STEVE. Right.

> *Little pause. Then, more small talk.*

KATHY. Spain's fantastic. We did four days in Barcelona. Saw the what's-it-called? The cathedral? Big, crazy – ?

TOM. Sagrada Familia.

KATHY. That. Which I loved. Likewise the food. Which I would happily eat every day for the rest of my life.

KEVIN. Paella.

KATHY. Then Morocco. To whatzit. To Marrakesh. Which – I don't know how you feel about *heat*? But oh my God. And they keep giving you *hot tea*. Like, how refreshing. And some theory about how you're supposed to *sweat* in order to feel *cool*, which you'll have to explain to me some time.

TOM (*to himself*). Hot in *here*.

LENA. *Very* hot.

KATHY. *And*. To top it off. I don't want to bore you with the whole ugly saga *but*: when they tell you not to eat the produce? Take heed.

KEVIN. Like Mexico.

KATHY. Because if you ever need to know where to find a doctor at two in the morning in the capital of Morocco when your husband is doubled over with *dysentery* – ?

KEVIN. Whoa.

KATHY. Gimme a call.

Little pause. All look at door.

TOM (*re:* LINDSEY*'s absence*). Said two seconds.

KEVIN (*to* KATHY, *indicating himself and* LENA). Went to *Prague* last April.

KATHY (*to* LENA). Oh, I *love* Prague. Prague is beautiful.

KEVIN. Very pretty.

KATHY. The architecture?

KEVIN. That bridge?

KATHY. And it's small, is what's nice. So you can do it all in a couple of days.

KEVIN. And then from there to Zurich.

KATHY. Never been to Switzerland. (*With a laugh.*) But I like the cheese!

LENA (*formally*). Can I – ? I'm sorry. I didn't mean to – but I was hoping I could say something to everyone, if you don't mind?

All pause for LENA.

As long as we're stopped?

KATHY. No. Do.   KEVIN. Go ahead.   TOM. Yeah yeah,
By all means.   please.

LENA. All right, well… (*Clears her throat.*) Um, I just feel like it's very important for me to express, before we start getting into the details –

STEVE. Sorry, but – maybe we should wait for Lindsey? Don't you think? If it's something important? Otherwise –

KEVIN (*to* LENA). Do you mind?

STEVE. Wind up repeating yourself.

TOM (*to* LENA). That okay with you?

LENA. It's fine with me.

STEVE. But, hold that thought.

LENA. I will.

Little pause. TOM *drums his fingers.*

STEVE. Meanwhile –

TOM. Meanwhile maybe we should look at page three?

KATHY. Maybe we should.

TOM. Catch her up when she – (*To* STEVE.) If that's cool with you guys.

STEVE. S'cool with me.

TOM. Good.

KEVIN. Let's do it.

TOM. Just cuz I gotta be outta here by like four.

STEVE. Forge ahead.

KATHY. Page three.

TOM. Middle of three.

KATHY. Section two.

TOM. Roman numeral two.

STEVE (*aside to* KATHY, *quietly*). Rabat, by the way.

    Beat.

TOM. Whadja say?

STEVE. Nothing.

KATHY. Couldn't hear you.

STEVE. The capital.

TOM. Of what?

STEVE. Morocco. She said Marrakesh.

KATHY. It *is* the capital.

STEVE. No.

TOM. I'd've said Marrakesh.

STEVE. Rabat.

KATHY. I don't think you're right.

STEVE. No, it is.

KATHY. But possibly.

STEVE. Definitely. Anyway.

TOM. Anyway –

KATHY. Or, wait. Is it *Tangiers*?

STEVE. Nope.

KATHY. Why am I thinking Tangiers?

STEVE. Dunno.

KATHY. Maybe we just *landed* in Tang – Or wait, no we didn't.

KEVIN (*to* STEVE). *What's* the capital?

KATHY. I know what it is. Tangiers was the *old* capital.

STEVE. Umm… no?

KATHY. The *historic* capital.

LINDSEY *returns*.

LINDSEY. *So* sorry.

KEVIN. Everything all right?

LINDSEY (*returning* KATHY*'s phone*). It's fine. It's just, he said he was going to be in Seattle so we went ahead and scheduled this without him and now he's feeling a little proprietary – Anyway. Blah blah.

TOM. So, we skipped ahead.

LINDSEY. Great.

TOM. To page three?

KATHY. Middle of three.

TOM. And since I think we'd all basically agree that –

STEVE (*to* LINDSEY). Hey. (*To* TOM.) Sorry. (*To* LINDSEY.) What's the capital of Morocco?

LINDSEY. The what?

STEVE. The capital.

LINDSEY. What are you talking about?

STEVE. Of Morocco.

LINDSEY. Why?

STEVE. Quick. Just –

LINDSEY. I have no idea.

STEVE. Yes you do.

KATHY (*explaining to* LINDSEY). I said Marrakesh.

STEVE (*to* KATHY). No no,   LINDSEY. Marrakesh, yeah.
    let her –

STEVE. No. *Rabat*.

LINDSEY. Whatever.

KEVIN (*explaining to* LINDSEY). Trying to figure out what it was.

LINDSEY. *Why?*

STEVE. She said she went to the capital of Morocco –

LINDSEY. So?

STEVE. – and it's not the capital.

LINDSEY (*with a shrug*). Maybe they changed it.

Beat, then:

STEVE. Who?

LINDSEY. The Moroccans.

STEVE. To what?

LINDSEY. Whatever it is now.

STEVE. Which is *Rabat*.

LINDSEY. Okay.

TOM. So –

KATHY. Oh, wait. You know what it is? It's *Timbuktu*.

STEVE.…*Nnnnnnno?*

KATHY. The old capital. The historic – (*Tapping her temple.*) That's why I – because it was part of our package.

STEVE. Um. Timbuktu is in *Mali*.

KATHY. But the *ancient* capital.

STEVE. Yeah. Of *Mali*.

LINDSEY. I thought Mali was in the Pacific.

STEVE (*baffled*). In – ?

LINDSEY. Where do they have the shadow puppets?

STEVE (*sputtering*). Are you talking about *Bali*?

KATHY. Same difference.

STEVE. Uhhhh, *no*? The *difference* – (*Continues*.)

LINDSEY (*overlapping*). And who *gives* a shit, any – ?
(*Continues*.)

DAN *has entered through the kitchen door. Work clothes,
moustache, chewing gum. He lingers at a distance.*

STEVE. – is that	LINDSEY. –	LENA. I'm sorry. I
they happen to	Steve. Steven.	don't mean to
be three distinct	It's whatever	interrupt
countries so, I	you want it to	anyone, but –
guess I give a	be, okay?	
shit –		
(*Continues*.)		

STEVE (*lowering his voice, to* LINDSEY). – and could you
possibly not talk to me like a *child*?

LENA (*in the clear*). Excuse me?

All turn to LENA.

I was hoping to say something, if I could?

STEVE (*remembering*). Oh oh oh.

TOM. Right. (*To* LENA.) Sorry. (*To* LINDSEY.) Lena had
wanted to mention something and it sounded kind of
important so –

KEVIN (*to* LENA). But you don't gotta ask *permission*.

LENA. I'm trying to be polite.

LINDSEY. We're totally rude.

KEVIN. No, you're not.

LINDSEY. It's my family. Irish Catholic, you know? *Blarney*.

KATHY (*raising a hand*). Please, my husband? Half-Jewish,
half-Italian.

KEVIN. Is that right?

KATHY. Get a word in edgewise.

KEVIN. I believe that.

KATHY. Anyway. Lena.

LENA. Thank you.

LINDSEY. Wait. *Lena*, right?

LENA. Lena.

KATHY. Short for Leonora?

LENA. No.

KATHY. I knew a Leonora.

LENA. It was my aunt's name.

LINDSEY (*reminding herself*). Anyway. Lena, Kevin.

KATHY (*raising hand*). Kathy.

LINDSEY (*indicating*). Kathy, Lindsey, Steve.

STEVE. And Tom.

KEVIN. Don't forget Tom.

LINDSEY. Tom we know. So:

DAN (*from across the room*). Ding dong?

   All turn to DAN.

STEVE. Hey.

DAN. Hey.

STEVE. How's it goin'?

DAN. S'there a Steve anywhere?

STEVE. Yeah?

DAN. You Steve?

STEVE. Yeah?

DAN. Hector said if there's a problem talk to Steve?

STEVE. That's me.

DAN (*to the others*). How ya doing?

TOM. Hey. Good.   KEVIN. Doing all   LENA. Fine, thank
                            right.   you.

DAN. Uhh… (*Lowers voice, crouches next to* STEVE.) Quick
    question?

STEVE (*a quiet sidebar*). Yeah?

DAN (*privately*). So okay. So, we're, uh, digging that trench
    back there, ya know?

STEVE. Yeah?

DAN. Out in back?

STEVE. Yeah?

DAN. For the conduit line?

STEVE. Yeah?

DAN. Know what I'm talking about?

STEVE. Yeah?

DAN. Cuz before you hook up that line you gotta bury that
    conduit?

STEVE. Yeah?

DAN. And so in order to dig that trench we gotta take out that
    tree, right?

STEVE. Right?

DAN. Dead tree back there?

STEVE. Yeah?

DAN. Cuz those roots, they go down like maybe eight feet?

STEVE. Yeah?

DAN. Which is why we're taking out that tree?

STEVE. Right?

DAN. Didja know that thing is *dead*?

STEVE (*rising*). Hey. Maybe we should – (*To the others.*) Sorry. You guys go ahead and –

DAN. Whoops.

STEVE (*to* DAN). No no. It's just – two things at once.

KEVIN. We can wait.

STEVE. No no no. You guys keep – (*To* DAN.) You wanna show me?

DAN. Lemme show ya.

STEVE. Lemme take a look.

DAN. Show ya what we're dealing with.

> DAN *and* STEVE *exit out the back door.*

> (*Overheard to* STEVE, *as they exit.*) Tell ya one thing though, it is hot out here.

> LENA *fans herself. A little pause, then:*

LINDSEY. Now I don't remember what we were – ?

TOM. Page three.

LINDSEY. *Right.*

KATHY. Middle of three.

TOM. So. Knowing as we do that the height continues to be the sticking point – and by the way, the reason the petition was drawn up this way in the first place – I mean, nobody wants to be inflexible, but the idea was to set some basic guidelines whereby *if*, say, the height is the problem, like it is here, then one option would be to reduce the total exterior volume, like your husband was saying. And that's the rationale behind the table at the bottom of the page. So what those figures mean, essentially, is that, with each additional foot of elevation beyond the maximum limit, there'd be a corresponding reduction in volume. And the numbers are based on the scale of the *original* structures, which is relatively consistent over the twelve-block radius, and of which this house is a fairly typical example. Now:

KATHY. Except we know they're *not*.

TOM. Not what?

KATHY. Not consistent.

TOM. Saying *relatively*.

KATHY. A lotta variables.

TOM. We know that.

KATHY (*beginning a list*). The size of the lots, for starters?

TOM. Right, but –

KATHY. The year of construction?

TOM. Right, so the hope was that, by establishing a couple of regulations up front, hopefully we avoid this kinda situation in the future, cuz, obviously, it's a pain in the ass for everybody. So, assuming the Landmarks Committee passes this part of the petition next week –

KATHY. *Assuming*.

TOM. Safe assumption.

KATHY. And if the Landmarks Committee really wants to pick that fight with the Zoning Department that is *their* business, but that's a matter of *if and when*.

TOM (*to* LINDSEY). Why is this confrontational?

KATHY. Because somebody might've raised these issues when the plans went to the Zoning Department five months ago.

LINDSEY. Kathy.

KATHY. I mean, no one had any objection back *then*.

LINDSEY. Can I say? We *talked* about renovation. We discussed it. Because these houses are *so* charming and I know it's a shame – but when you figure in the crack in the subfloor and the cost of the lead abatement – and in a market like this one? It just made more sense to start from scratch.

TOM*'s cellphone rings. He tries to ignore it.*

TOM. Right. *But*: the Owners Association has a vested interest
   – Kevin and Lena call me up last month, they say Tom,
   we've got this problem, these people are planning to build a
   house that's a full fifteen feet taller than all the adjacent
   structures – (*Continues.*)

LINDSEY. Nooo… *fifteen?* Is   KATHY. It's exactly what the
   that right?   block is zoned for, Tom.

TOM. – and I think we'd *all* agree that there's a mutual benefit
   to maintaining the integrity – (*Glances at his phone.*) the
   architectural integrity –

LINDSEY. Wanna get that?

TOM. – of a historically significant – God damn it – neighbourhood. (*Answering phone.*) Yeah?

   STEVE *returns, as* TOM *talks, leaving the kitchen door
   open.*

   (*On phone.*) Yeah, okay, but don't call me with that in the
   middle of a Satur – ? Well, then give it to Marla. Because it's
   Marla's account. Well, where the fuck is Mar – ? (*To the
   others.*) Sorry.

   TOM *crosses the room to take the call.*

STEVE. What's happening?

LINDSEY. I don't know.

LENA. You know, it might be a good idea if we all turned off
   our phones.

LINDSEY. Excellent idea.

KEVIN (*to* STEVE). Get your problem solved?

STEVE. Did what?

KEVIN. Out back.

STEVE. Yeah, I dunno. They hit something.

LINDSEY. What something?

STEVE. I dunno.

LINDSEY. Something dangerous?

STEVE. I dunno.

LINDSEY. Is it going to *explode*?

STEVE. It's not – (*To* KEVIN.) We're putting in a koi pond, and there's a filtration system that has to hook into the municipal – anyway, they ran into some kind of – whatever. So whatzit, page three?

KEVIN. But maybe wait for Tom?

STEVE (*with a laugh and a shrug*)….Standing right *there*.

KEVIN. If we're getting into the legal stuff?

LINDSEY. I agree.

KEVIN. Cuz, I'm not a lawyer.

STEVE. I'm not a lawyer.

LINDSEY. But, Kathy's a lawyer.

STEVE (*re:* TOM). And he's the one with the time issue.

KEVIN. Long as we're out by four.

STEVE (*'okay, but…'*). It's three thirty.

KATHY. We'll be done by four.

LINDSEY (*to* KEVIN *and* LENA). Sorry about all this.

STEVE. Crazy.

All turn vaguely to TOM, *who gestures apologetically and mouths 'Sorry'.* LENA *sighs, fans herself.*

KEVIN (*small talk*). When's the baby due?

LINDSEY. Oh. Um, November.

KEVIN. In time for turkey.

LINDSEY. I know.

KEVIN. Boy or girl?

STEVE is about to answer.

LINDSEY. No no no. I don't want to know. Ask Steve. Steve saw the ultrasound. (*Fingers in ears, eyes closed.*) La la la la la la la la la la la – (*Continues.*)

STEVE *mouths the word 'Boy', then touches* LINDSEY'*s knee.*

(*Fingers out of ears, eyes open.*) – la la la – either way as long as it's healthy.

KEVIN. Knock wood.

LINDSEY. But something tells me it's a girl.

Pause. Feet tap. KATHY *takes out her phone, dials a number, listens.*

(*To* LENA.) You guys have kids?

LENA. Three.

LINDSEY. Wow.

LENA. Mmm.

LINDSEY. How great for you.

LENA. Yes.

LINDSEY. Congratulations.

LENA. Thank you.

KATHY *starts to check her messages.*

Beat, then:

STEVE (*to* KEVIN). So, Kyle Hendrickson?

KEVIN (*remembering*). Kyle Hendrickson.

STEVE. Kyle Hendrickson – *who*, may I add, kicked my ass in the tenth grade?

LINDSEY. *Who* is this?

KEVIN (*laughing*). Wait wait wait. *Little* Kyle Hendrickson – ?

STEVE. Like the *one* solitary black dude in my entire high school.

KEVIN. Kicked *your* ass?

STEVE. *Publicly* kicked.

KEVIN. Kyle Hendrickson's like, what? Like five-*two*?

LINDSEY. Wait. *When?*

STEVE (*to* KEVIN). Five-five. J.V. Wrestling team. Tenth grade.

KEVIN. I think that might officially make you – ?

STEVE. A pussy?

KEVIN. Think it might.

LINDSEY (*to* STEVE). *Who* are you talking about?

STEVE. Okay. Remember I ran into a guy?

LINDSEY. No.

STEVE. Remember last week? I said a guy from middle school?

LINDSEY. No.

STEVE. I was meeting you downtown – oh, and he told me the *joke*?

LINDSEY. Right?

STEVE. The joke I told you?

LINDSEY. I don't remember.

STEVE. The joke about – well, neither do I, at the moment but it was a joke we both thought was funny?

LINDSEY. Okay?

STEVE. Anyway. *That* guy: *that* is Kyle Hendrickson. Who *he* works with.

LINDSEY (*to* LENA). Glad we cleared *that* up.

STEVE. Oh oh oh.

LINDSEY. What?

STEVE. Wait.

LINDSEY. What?

STEVE. Wait.

LINDSEY. *What?*

STEVE. The joke. It's about a guy? Remember? Guy who goes to jail?

LINDSEY. No.

STEVE. White-collar criminal goes to jail, remember? And and and they put him in a cell with – ?

LINDSEY (*realising, privately to* STEVE). *Oh* oh oh. No.

STEVE. What?

LINDSEY. Hm-mm.

STEVE. *What?*

LINDSEY. Let's – (*Changing subject, to* LENA.) How old are your kids?

STEVE (*to* LINDSEY). What'samatter?

KEVIN (*to* LINDSEY). Nine, ten and twelve.

LINDSEY. *Wow*.

STEVE (*to* LINDSEY). What's your problem?

LINDSEY. Steve.

STEVE. I was telling the joke.

LINDSEY. Later.

STEVE. You said remind me what joke –

LINDSEY. Okay.

STEVE (*laughing*). But now I'm not *allowed* to tell it?

LINDSEY (*quietly*). Stop a second.

STEVE (*to* KEVIN). Anyway. Two guys stuck in a jail cell –

LINDSEY. *Steven?*

LENA (*finally having had enough*). I'm sorry, and I don't mean to keep interrupting but can somebody please explain to me what it is we're *doing* here?

Pause. TOM *turns. All feel the chill from* LENA.

TOM (*quietly, on phone*). Just send me the fucking document.

KATHY *and* TOM *discreetly hang up their respective phones.*

LENA. I mean, I know I'm not the only person who takes the situation seriously and I don't like having to be this way but I have been sitting here for the last fifteen minutes waiting for a turn to speak – (*Continues.*)

All, quietly chastened.

TOM. Hey. Sorry 'bout that.	KEVIN. No one's taking *turns*.	LINDSEY. I'm so sorry. I really am.	KATHY. Well, Tom was on the phone, I thought.

LENA. – and meanwhile it seems like nothing is even remotely getting accomplished –

LINDSEY. I agree.

A truck horn sounds outside.

KEVIN (*to* LENA). So go ahead and say what you –

LENA (*with a tense smile, to* KEVIN). And could you please not tell me when to – ?

KEVIN. I'm not telling –

LENA. They were having a conversation and – (*Continues.*)

KEVIN (*overlapping*). And now they stopped.

LENA. – I try not to intrude – (*Continues.*)

KEVIN. Just being friendly.

LENA. – on other people's conversations when they're in the middle of them. (*To the others.*) I'm not trying to be unfriendly.

LINDSEY. No, it's us.

KEVIN. No it's not.

LINDSEY. No, it is.

KEVIN. You're being friendly.

LENA. *I'm* being friendly.

LINDSEY (*to* KEVIN, *re:* LENA). She's being friendly.

STEVE. *I'm* being friendly.

KEVIN. If anybody's not being friendly –

LENA. Well, maybe the *friendly* thing to do would be for us to respect each other's time, would that be all right?

STEVE.	LINDSEY.	KATHY.	TOM.
Yeah. Sure.	*Yes*.	Was it me?	Sorry.
	Totally.	Was it?	Really.

LENA. Thank you.

All murmur quietly.

STEVE (*to*	LINDSEY.	KATHY.	TOM.
KEVIN).	*So* glad	Cuz, seri-	No, you
Was I *dis-*	someone	ously, I	guys? Was
repectful?	has the	thought	my fault.
	balls to	we'd	That was
	finally *say*	stopped.	me.
	it.		

Horn sounds again.

LINDSEY (*to* LENA). Anyway.

LENA. Anyway. All right. (*Taking her time.*) Well… I have no way of knowing what sort of connection you have to the neighbourhood where *you* grew up?

Horn again. STEVE *turns.*

LINDSEY (*to* STEVE, *rapid whisper*). *Just shut the door. Just shut the fucking –*

STEVE *jumps up to shut the kitchen door.*

Sorry. (*Prompting, continuing* LENA's *last line.*) The neighbourhood where – ?

LENA. And some of our concerns have to do with a particular period in history and the things that people experienced here in this community *during* that period – (*Continues.*)

STEVE *returns to the circle, sits.*

STEVE (*whispering to* LENA). Sorry.

LENA. – both good and bad, and on a personal level? I just have a lot of *respect* for the people who went through those experiences and still managed to carve out a life for themselves and create a community despite a whole lot of obstacles?

LINDSEY. As well you should.

LENA. Some of which still exist. That's just a part of my *history* and my *parents'* history – and honouring the *connection* to that history – and, *no one*, myself included, likes having to dictate what you can or can't do with your own home, but there's just a lot of *pride*, and a lot of *memories* in these houses, and for some of us, that connection still has *value*, if that makes any sense?

LINDSEY. Total sense.

LENA. For those of us who have remained.

LINDSEY. Absolutely.

LENA. And *respecting* that memory: that has value, too. At least, that's what *I* believe. And that's what I've been wanting to say.

All nod solemnly for several seconds at LENA's *noble speech.*

STEVE. Um. Can I ask a – ?

LINDSEY (*to* STEVE).	STEVE (*to* LENA).
Let her finish.	Sorry.

LENA. I was finished.

LINDSEY (*to* LENA). Sorry.

STEVE. Right. So, um… Huh. (*'How to say it?'*) So, when you use the word *value*, um – ?

LENA. Historical value.

TOM. You read the petition.

STEVE. Yeah.

TOM. Spelled out pretty clearly.

STEVE. Right. (*To* LENA.) But, what I mean is – So, you don't literally mean… *monetary* value. Right?

LENA *stares*.

LENA. My great-aunt – (*Continues.*)

STEVE. Or maybe you do.

LENA. – was one of the first people of colour to – in a sense, she was a pioneer –

STEVE. No, I understand – and correct me if – but *my* understanding was that the value of these properties had gone *up*.

KATHY. They have.

STEVE (*to* KEVIN *and* LENA). Yours included.

KEVIN. That's true.

STEVE. *Way* up.

TOM. And we'd all like to *keep* it that way.

STEVE. But – You're not suggesting, are you, that, when we build *our* house – ?

LINDSEY *puts a hand on* STEVE.

LINDSEY (*to* LENA). Look, I for one – I am really grateful for what you said, but this is why we sometimes feel defensive, you know? Because we *love* this neighbourhood.

STEVE. We do.

LINDSEY. We completely do, and we would never want to to to to carelessly – (*Continues*.)

STEVE. Run roughshod.

LINDSEY. – over anyone's – And I totally admit, I'm the one who was resistant, especially with the schools and everything, but once I stopped seeing the neighbourhood the way it *used* to be, and could see what it is *now*, and its *potential*?

LENA. Used to be what?

LINDSEY. What do you mean?

LENA. What it used to be?

STEVE (*helpfully, to* LENA). What *you* said. About the *history* of – ?

LINDSEY. *Historically*. The changing, you know, demographic – ?

STEVE. Although *originally* – (*To* LINDSEY.) Wasn't it German, predominantly?

KATHY. German and Irish.

STEVE. Depending how far back you –

KATHY. It's funny, though. Even though my father was German – but back when they were living here –

LINDSEY. Wait, did I know this?

KATHY. I told you that.

LINDSEY. In this neighbourhood?

KATHY (*to* KEVIN *and* LENA). They went to church at St Stan's! Isn't that crazy?

KEVIN. Is that right?

KATHY (*to* KEVIN *and* LENA). This is the late fifties. (*Laugh*.) My father was a 'Rotarian'! But my *mother* – (*To* LINDSEY.) She was deaf? I told you that?

LINDSEY. *That* I knew.

KEVIN. Awwwww, that's a shame.

KATHY (*to* KEVIN). Thank you. It was congenital. But then she got pregnant with me and they moved out to Rosemont, anyway, *her* family, *they* were Swedish.

STEVE (*to* KEVIN *and* LENA). There was a great article two weeks ago – I don't know if you saw this – about the history of the changing, uh, ethnic –

LINDSEY. Distribution.

LENA. Oh, I should read that.

STEVE. Of the neighbourhood and how in the seventies, eighties, how that was followed by a period of – of – of – of – of rapid –

KATHY. Decline.

LINDSEY.	STEVE.	KATHY.
No – Not – No –	Of *growth*. A growing –	I don't mean *decline* – (*Continues*.)

KATHY. – I mean there was *trouble*.

LINDSEY. Not *trouble*, she didn't mean –

KEVIN. There was trouble.

LINDSEY. *Economic* trouble.

KEVIN. Violence is trouble.

KATHY. That's what I'm saying.

KEVIN. Drugs are trouble.

KATHY (*vindicated*). Exactly.

LINDSEY. And the violence as an *outgrowth* of the criminalisation of those drugs.

KEVIN (*re: himself and* LENA). Cuz ya know, the two of us wuz both crackheads.

A frozen moment, then:

STEVE.	LINDSEY.	KATHY.	KEVIN
That's funny. I know you're kidding but that *was* the percep-tion at the time.	No, come on. Don't say that. Really. Even as a joke.	I know you're joking, but that is exactly what people *thought*.	(*laughs*). I'm kidding you. I'm just messing with you.

STEVE (*to* LINDSEY). He's being *funny*.

LINDSEY. I know he was, and it was funny but when people are systematically *dehumanised* – If you've been placed in some faceless, institutional –

KATHY (*explaining to* KEVIN *and* LENA). The projects.

LINDSEY. I mean, like it or not, that kind of environment is not conducive to – to – to – to –

KEVIN. That's true.

LINDSEY. – the formation of *community*.

KATHY. Horrible.

KEVIN. Tough place to grow up.

LINDSEY. With the effect on *children*?

KEVIN. On anyone.

LINDSEY. And to take what had been a pros – well, not prosperous, but a solidly middle-class, um – ?

STEVE. Enclave.

LINDSEY. And then *undermine* the entire economic –

STEVE. Infrastructure.

LINDSEY. – by *warehousing* people inside of these –

STEVE. But that's the thing, right? If you construct some artificial *semblance* of a community, and then isolate people *within* that – I mean, what would be the definition of a *ghetto*, you know? A ghetto is a place where – (*Continues*.)

LINDSEY (*overlapping, to* STEVE). But who *uses* that word? I don't.

STEVE. – where, where, where people are *sequestered*, right? (*To* LINDSEY, *defensively*.) The *definition*, I'm saying.

LENA. Well, *my* family –

STEVE. Like Prague. If you think of – (*Pedagogically*.) Okay: Prague had this ghetto, right? A Jewish ghetto?

LENA (*'thanks for the lecture'*). We've been to Prague.

LINDSEY. Ohmigod. Prague is beautiful.

KEVIN *wiggles his hand*.

I loved Pr – you didn't love it?

KEVIN. Prague's *crowded*.

KATHY. And the food sucks. Or is that just me?

STEVE (*with a laugh*). But I'm saying, it's not like, one day all these Jews were sitting around Prague, looking at the real-estate section, going, *Hey here's an idea! Let's all go live in that ghetto!* Right?

A beat where they all avoid STEVE*'s comment. Then:*

LINDSEY (*to* LENA). When were you in Prague?

LENA. Last April.

KEVIN. First Prague, then Zurich.

LINDSEY. I want to go back.

KEVIN (*to* STEVE). You ski?

A laugh erupts from LINDSEY.

LINDSEY (*re:* STEVE). *Him?*

STEVE. You mean – like *downhill*?

LINDSEY. *That* I'd like to see.

KEVIN. Ever been to Switzerland?

STEVE (*to* LINDSEY, *defensive*). I can *ski*. I *have* skied.

LINDSEY. Get that on video.

STEVE. Why is that funny?

LINDSEY (*trying not to laugh, to* KEVIN). Sorry.

STEVE. Seriously. What is it about the idea of me skiing that
    you find so highly, uh – ?

LINDSEY. Anyway.

STEVE. – *risible?*

KEVIN (*to* STEVE). I just meant, you like to golf, you go to
    Scotland. And if you like to *ski*?

LINDSEY (*still laughing*). Just trying to picture it.

STEVE. Gratuitous.

TOM (*prodding the others*). Annnnnnyway.

LENA. Yes. Maybe we should try to stick to the topic at hand.	LINDSEY. Okay. Tom's right. Let's get it together.	KATHY (*to* KEVIN). I can't ski because I was born with weak ankles. Anyway.

LINDSEY (*to* TOM). *Where* were we?

TOM. Page three.

LINDSEY. Ugh. You're kidding.

TOM. Nope.

LINDSEY. How can we still be – ?

TOM. I dunno.

LINDSEY. How is that possible?

TOM (*glancing at watch*). And it is now… quarter to four.

LENA. And I'm sorry for taking time.

LINDSEY. No. What you said was *great*.

LENA. I wasn't trying to *romanticise*.

LINDSEY. You didn't.

LENA. Nothing *romantic* about being poor.

LINDSEY. But, it was your *neighbourhood*.

KATHY (*to* LENA). Wait, what street?

LENA. Offa Larabee.

KATHY. My parents lived on Claremont!!

KEVIN. Y'all would've been neighbours.

LENA. But I didn't mean to make it about my personal *connection* to the house. It's more about the *principle*.

KEVIN. But you can't *live* in a *principle*.

LINDSEY. You had a personal connection?

KEVIN. To the house.

LINDSEY. To *this* house?

KEVIN (*to* LINDSEY). Her aunt.

LENA. I don't want to – let's not.

KEVIN. Lived here.

STEVE. Wait. *Who?*

LENA. Sort of beside the point, but yes.

KEVIN. *Great*-aunt –

LENA. On my mother's side.

LINDSEY. You don't mean, *here*, here?

LENA. And this is fifty years ago.

LINDSEY. Here in this *house*.

LENA. For quite some time, actually.

LINDSEY (*hand to her*   STEVE. *Whoa*.
heart). Oh my g – ! So so
so wait, so – ?

STEVE (*clarifying*). This *exact house*.

LINDSEY (*'how weird'*). So, like, you've... *been in this room*?

LENA. I used to climb a tree in the backyard.

LINDSEY. Oh my God.   STEVE. Whoa.

LENA. A crepe myrtle tree?

KATHY. Well, that is just bizarre.

KEVIN. Any rate, her great-aunt – and she had to save a long
time to be able to afford a house like this.

LENA. She was a domestic worker.

   LINDSEY *and* KATHY *make quiet expressions of sympathy.*

KEVIN. And, a house isn't cheap –

LENA. Not *here*, anyway.

KEVIN. Here at *that* time.

LENA. At *that* time – Well, when *I* was growing up I really
don't remember seeing a single white face in the neighbourhood for pretty much my entire –

KEVIN. Well, one, you said.

LENA. Who?

KEVIN. What's his name?

LENA. Mr Wheeler?

KEVIN. Mr Wheeler.

LENA (*to the others*). I don't think anybody knew his first
name.

KEVIN. He was a... what?

LENA (*to* LINDSEY). At the grocery store.

KEVIN. Bagged the groceries.

LENA. At the Sup'r – Well, back then it was Gelman's but they tore down Gelman's.

KEVIN. And that became Sup'r Sav'r?

LENA. Well, then they tore down Sup'r Sav'r, so –

KEVIN. You know where the Whole Foods is?

STEVE (*with a laugh*). And what happened to Mr Wheeler?

KEVIN. Dead, probably.

LENA. He was, you know… (*Touches her head*.) developmentally…?

LINDSEY.	STEVE.	KATHY.
Ohhhh. That's so sad.	Huh. Wow. Depressing.	Ohhhh… you know why that upsets me? I have a niece with Asperger's Syndrome.

LENA. But, given the make-up of the neighbourhood at that time and the price of a home like this one, the question naturally arises as to whether it was the thing that happened here in the house – whether that in some way –

KEVIN. Played a factor.

LENA. – in making a place like this affordable. For a person of her income.

All stare. Pause.

STEVE. The *thing*.

LENA. The sad – you know.

LINDSEY. I don't.

LENA. The tragic –

KEVIN. Thing that happened.

LINDSEY. What thing?

KEVIN (*'no big deal'*). Well. Long time ago, but –

STEVE. In *this* house?

LENA. I'm just saying that, since she was one of the very first people of colour –

LINDSEY. Wait. Something happened in the house?

STEVE. What, somebody *died*, or – ?

KEVIN. S'not important.

LINDSEY. That we should be concerned about?

KEVIN. No no no no no.

LENA. Just that – there'd *been* a family. Who had a son who'd been in the Army.

KEVIN. Korea, maybe?

LENA. And who, well, a few years after he came back from the war –

KEVIN. Killed himself.

Beat.

LINDSEY. Oh my God.

KEVIN. Yeah.

STEVE. Wow.

LINDSEY. *Oh* my God.

KEVIN. Sad.

STEVE. Wow.

LINDSEY. Oh my God.

LENA. Which my great-aunt didn't know at the time.

LINDSEY. Oh my God, that is just –

LENA. Though I assumed you *did*.

STEVE. Umm, no?

LINDSEY. That is just – just – just – Wait. And they went ahead and *sold* the house to – ?

LENA. Mm-hmm.

STEVE. Wow.

LINDSEY. Without *telling* her that? Because nobody ever told *us* that.

KATHY. Well, they *wouldn't*, would they?

KEVIN (*dismissive*). Fifty *years* ago.

LINDSEY (*to* KATHY). But *legally*, I mean, don't you have to *tell* people that?

KATHY. Not if you want to sell it.

LENA. It was something like he'd come back from the Army. And he'd been accused of something.

KEVIN. Killing people.

LENA. Innocent people.

KEVIN. Killing civilians.

LENA. And then – you know – *himself*.

STEVE. But you don't mean, like like like like… (*Laughs.*) Like *here in this very* – ?

LENA (*laughing along with* STEVE). No – I mean, not *where we're sitting*.

KEVIN. Upstairs, wasn't it?

LINDSEY (*freaking out*). I – I – I – I –

STEVE (*touching* LINDSEY). Breathe.

LINDSEY (*pushing* STEVE's *hand away*). Stop it.

LENA. I mean, the version *I* was told was, that he went upstairs.

KEVIN. Hanged himself.

LINDSEY (*standing*). Okay. *No*. No, I'm sorry, but that is *wrong*.

STEVE. Where are you going?

LINDSEY walks out of the room. STEVE follows her. From off, we hear:

LINDSEY. That is just – *No*. To sell someone a – a – a *house*, where – ?

STEVE. What'samatter?

LINDSEY (*somewhat privately*). *No*. There should be a *law*. And I don't care *how*, okay? I don't want to know *how* he did it or in *what room* – Because I'm sorry, but that is just something that, from a legal standpoint, you should have to *tell* people!

KATHY (*calling to* LINDSEY). It's not.

LINDSEY (*sticking her head back in, to* KATHY). *Well, it fucking well should be.*

STEVE. Hey. Hey.

LINDSEY (*privately, to* STEVE). And now I have this horrifying *image* in my head?

STEVE (*to* LINDSEY, *laughing*). But why d'you have to make such a big deal outta – ?

LINDSEY. Uh, it *is* a big deal, Steve. If your *child* – if *our family* is going to live in a house where – ?

STEVE (*laughing, to the others*). I mean, it's not like he's still hanging up there!

LINDSEY (*losing her shit, to* STEVE). *It's not funny, okay?!! It's not funny to me, so why are you acting like an asshole?!!*

The kitchen door bangs open and DAN *noisily enters.*

DAN (*calling out*). *Okay*. Show ya whatcha got.

He drags a large trunk – the footlocker we saw in Act One, covered with mould and dirt – into the middle of the room.

So that's your problem, right there. (*Coughs a couple of times.*) 'Scuse me. And I tell ya one thing: yank this up from down there, take a look at it, you know the first thing I'm thinking to myself? You know what I'm thinking? Buried treasure. Like Spanish doubloons or something and I know you're thinking Dan ya crazy bastard but I tell ya what. I know a guy.

He joins the circle.

(*Coughs again.*) 'Scuse me. This guy. Last summer he's taking out a septic system – this house out in Mundelein. He's sitting on top of his backhoe. All of a sudden, *clang*. And this guy's not exactly the sharpest tool in the box, if ya know what I mean, but he goes down in there about five, six feet with a chain and a winch – swear to God – ya know what he pulls out from down there? He stands back. He takes a look – (*Without stopping.*) You're in the middle of something.

STEVE. Sorta.

DAN. My bad.

STEVE. No no.

DAN. Bull in a china shop.

STEVE. It's cool.

DAN. According to my wife.

STEVE. Oh yeah?

DAN. As well as a couple other names not suitable for mixed – Anyways.

STEVE. Thanks

DAN (*re: the trunk*). I'll just leave this here for ya.

STEVE. Thank you.

DAN. Need me to open it, you lemme know.

STEVE. Great.

DAN. Problem, though. (*Indicating the large padlock.*) Problem's this puppy right here. Now the deal is: I got a saw. Take a hacksaw you could maybe saw it off but whatcha really want is a pair of bolt cutters and I don't think I got any bolt cutters, so.

STEVE. Ah, well.

DAN. Cuz you never know. Turns out to be fulla Spanish doubloons we'll haveta split it six ways, huh?

LINDSEY (*to* DAN, *taking over*). Sorry.

DAN. Whoops.

LINDSEY. I don't know your name.

DAN (*extending hand*). Dan.

LINDSEY. Hi, Dan.

DAN. Dan or Danny.

LINDSEY. Great.

DAN. *Daniel* when the wife gets pissed.

LINDSEY. But listen –

DAN. No no no no no no I gotcha.

LINDSEY. If you wouldn't mind?

DAN. Middle of your thing and I come barging right into –

LINDSEY. Thank you.

DAN. But you findya some bolt cutters you'll be in business.

LINDSEY. We will.

DAN (*an idea*). Hey, ya know what? Hang on a second.

DAN *heads to the back door. As he does:*

TOM. So I'm just going to push ahead, if that's okay?

DAN (*calling out the door, top of his lungs*). *Ramirez!!!*

TOM. Cuz we still got seventeen pages to cover –

LINDSEY (*to the others*). And I'm sorry I lost my shit. No, I did. But I think we're both wound a little tight right now with the baby and the house and the money and everything –

DAN. *Ramirez!!*

LINDSEY. – And then to top it all off, we get sent this petition in the mail, you know, and suddenly our entire lives are thrown into chaos at the very same moment that – I mean, the demolition was scheduled to start on Monday and unless we get this resolved which I want as much as anyone then what do people expect?

DAN. *Ram – !!!* Ah, screw it.

DAN *gives up, exits.*

TOM (*continuing*). So: couple of options. One, as we said, is reducing the height –

KATHY (*adamantly*). No. Tom, I'm sorry, but you can't just call an architect at the eleventh hour and snap your fingers and say can you completely redesign an entire –

LINDSEY. It's a little late in the day for that.

LENA (*to* LINDSEY). I'm sorry you're upset.

LINDSEY. I'm not upset. I'm not.

KATHY. And may I remind everybody that these guys are under no obligation, legal *or* otherwise –

TOM (*from a document*). Okay. Here's the wording from the City Council, and I quote: In recognition of the *historic* status of the Clybourne Park neighbourhood, and its distinctive collection of *low-rise single-family homes* – (*Continues.*)

| LINDSEY. Aren't we a single family? | KEVIN. Hey. Hey. Everything's cool. | TOM. – *intended to house a community of working-class families.* |

LINDSEY. And you know, the thing is? Communities change.

STEVE. They do.

LINDSEY. That's just the reality.

STEVE. It is.

LENA. And some change is inevitable, and we all support that, but it might be worth asking yourself who exactly is *responsible* for that change?

Little pause.

LINDSEY. I'm not sure what you – ?

KEVIN. Wait, what are you trying to – ?

LENA. I'm asking you to think about the motivation behind the long-range political initiative to change the face of this neighbourhood.

Another little pause.

LINDSEY. What does that mean? (*To* STEVE.) Do you know what – ?

STEVE (*to* LENA). Wait, say that again?

KEVIN. The long-range *what*?

LENA. I mean that this is a highly desirable area.

STEVE. Well, *we* desire it.

LENA. I know you do.

LINDSEY. Same as you.

LENA. And now the area is *changing*.

KATHY. And for the *better*, right?

LENA. And I'm saying that there are certain economic interests that are being served by those changes and others that are not. That's all.

STEVE (*suspiciously*). And… *which* interests are being – ?

LENA (*systematically*). If you have a residential area, in direct proximity to *downtown*?

STEVE. Right?

LENA. And if that area is occupied by a particular *group*?

STEVE. Which group?

LINDSEY (*to* LENA). You know what? We're talking about *one house*.

LENA (*to* LINDSEY). I understand that.

STEVE. Which group?

LINDSEY. A house for our family?

STEVE. Which group?

LENA. That's how it happens.

LINDSEY. In which to raise our *child*?

STEVE. No no. Which group?

LENA. It happens one house at a time.

STEVE. Whoa whoa whoa. Okay. Stop right there.

LINDSEY. What are you doing?

STEVE. No. I'm sorry, but can we just come out and *say* what it is we're actually – ? Shouldn't we maybe *do* that? Because if *that's* what this is really about, then… Jesus, maybe we oughta save ourselves some time and and and and just… *say* what it is we're really *saying* instead of doing this elaborate little *dance* around it?

Dead stop. All stare at STEVE.

Never mind.

KATHY. *What* dance?

STEVE. I – I – I – I shouldn't have – whatever.

LENA (*parsing his meaning*). So… you think I haven't been *saying* what I *actually* – ?

STEVE (*laughs*). Uhhh… Not to my way of thinking, no.

LENA. Well, what is it you *think* I'm – ?

STEVE. I – I – I… (*Laughs incredulously.*) Like we don't all *know*?

LINDSEY. *I* don't.

STEVE. Oh, *yes you do*. Of *course* you do.

KEVIN. Well, maybe you oughta *tell* us what *you* think she was saying.

STEVE. Oh oh, but it has to be *me*?

LENA. Well, you're the one who raised the question as to – (*Continues.*)

STEVE (*overlapping, laughs*). Oh, *come on*. It was *blatant*.

LENA. – the sincerity of my speech.

LINDSEY. What the fuck, Steve?

STEVE. You know what? Forget I said it.

LINDSEY. You didn't *say* anything.	LENA. Oh no, I'm *interested*.	STEVE. Let's forget the whole – (*Continues.*)

STEVE . – Okay. Okay. If you really want to – It's… (*Tries to laugh, then, sotto.*) It's *race*. Isn't it? You're trying to tell me that that… (*To* LENA.) That implicit in what you *said* – That this entire conversation… isn't at least *partly* informed – *Am I right?* (*Laughs nervously, to* LENA.) By the issue of… (*Sotto.*) of *racism*?

Beat, then:

LINDSEY (*to* STEVE). *Are you out of your* – ? (*To* LENA.) I have no idea where this is coming from.	STEVE (*to* LINDSEY). And *please* don't do that to me, okay? I've asked you repeatedly.

LENA. Well, the *original* issue was the inappropriately large *house* that – (*Continues.*)

STEVE (*to* LENA, *overlapping*). Oh, come on.

LENA. – you're planning to build. Only, *now* I'm fairly certain that I've been called a *racist*.

STEVE. But I didn't say that, did I?

LENA. *Sounded* like you did.

STEVE (*to* KEVIN). Did I say that?

KEVIN. Yeah, you kinda did.

STEVE. In what way did I say that?

KEVIN. Uh, *somebody* said racism.

STEVE. *Cism! – Cism!* Not – *cist*!!

KEVIN. Which must originate from *somewhere*.

STEVE. And which we all find totally reprehensi –

KEVIN. So – are *you* the racist?

STEVE. Can I just – ?

KEVIN. Is it your wife?

KATHY. Don't look at *me*.

STEVE. Look:

KEVIN. Cuz, by process of elimination –

STEVE. Here's what I'm saying:

LINDSEY. What *are* you saying?!

STEVE. I'm saying: was race *not* a factor –

LINDSEY (*re:* STEVE, *exonerating herself*). I don't know this person.

STEVE. Were there *not* these differences –

LINDSEY. *What* differences!!? There's no –

STEVE (*to* LINDSEY, *re:* LENA). Okay: she walks in here, from the very beginning, with all these issues – (*Continues.*)

LENA (*overlapping*). About your *house*.

STEVE. – and I'm only asking whether, were we not, shall we say – ?

LINDSEY. You're *creating* an issue. *Where none exists.*

STEVE. Oh oh oh you *heard* what she *said*. She as much as claimed that there's some kind of, of, of *secret conspiracy* –

LENA. Oh, it's not a *secret*.

| KEVIN (*to* LENA). Ohh, c'mon. Are you seriously – ? | LENA (*to* KEVIN). Oh, please don't be purposely naive. | STEVE. *There. Thank you. Now you see what I'm – ?* |

LENA. This has been under discussion for at least *four decades* now – (*Continues.*)

KEVIN (*overlapping, to* LENA). *You can't prove that.*

LENA. – at the highest institutional levels of – (*To* KEVIN.) Oh, don't act like you don't know it's true.

STEVE (*to* LENA). What, and now we're the evil invaders who are –

LINDSEY (*to* STEVE). *She never said that!!!!*

STEVE. – appropriating your *ancestral homeland?*

LINDSEY (*to* STEVE). This, this, this – No. I'm sorry, this is the most asinine – (*Sweetly, to* LENA *and* KEVIN.) *Half of my friends are black!*

STEVE (*sputtering*). What!!??

LINDSEY (*to* STEVE, *as to a child*). As is true for most *normal* people.

STEVE. Name *one*.

LINDSEY. *Normal* people? Tend to have *many* friends of a diverse and wide-ranging –

STEVE. You can't name *one*!

LINDSEY. Candace.

   Beat, then:

STEVE. Name another.

LINDSEY. *I don't have to stand here compiling a list of –*

STEVE. You said *half*. You *specifically –*

LINDSEY. Theresa.

STEVE. *She works in your office!! She's not your friend.*

LINDSEY. *She was at the baby shower, Steve! I hope she's not my enemy!!*

TOM. Well, this is all fascinating –

STEVE (*to* LINDSEY). Name another.

TOM. And while I'd love to sit here and review *all* of American History *maybe* we should concentrate on the plans for your property – (*Continues.*)

STEVE. Yes!! Yes!!   TOM. – which *had* been the
(*Continues.*)   *original* topic of the
                                  convers –

STEVE. – The history of America *is* the history of private property.

LENA. That may be –

STEVE. Read de Tocqueville.

LENA. Though I rather doubt *your* grandparents were *sold* as private property.

STEVE (*to* KEVIN *and* LENA). Ohhhhh my *God*. Look. Look. Humans are *territorial*, okay? (*Continues.*)

LINDSEY (*overlapping, to* STEVE). Who are you?

STEVE. – This is why we have *wars*. One group, one *tribe*, tries to usurp some territory – and now *you guys* have this territory, right? And you don't like having it *stolen away* from you, the way white people stole everything else from black America. *We get it*, okay? And we *apologise*. But what *good* does it do, if we perpetually fall into the same, predictable little euphemistic tap dance around the topic?

KEVIN. You know how to *tap dance*?

STEVE. *See? See what he's doing?!!*

LINDSEY. Maybe quit while you're ahead.

STEVE. *No.* I'm sick of – *No.* Every single word we say is – is – is *scrutinised* for some kind of latent – Meanwhile you guys run around saying N-word this and N-word that and *whatever.* We all know why there's a double standard but I can't even so much as repeat a fucking *joke* that the *one black guy I know told me* –

KEVIN. *So tell the goddamn joke.*

STEVE. Not *now*!!

KEVIN. If you feel so *oppressed*, either go ahead and *tell it* – (*Continues.*)

LINDSEY (*overlapping, to* STEVE). *Do not.*

KEVIN. – or maybe you could *move on.*

LINDSEY (*with finality*). *Thank you!*

LENA. Well, I want to hear it.

KEVIN (*to* LENA). Ohh, don't.	LENA (*to* KEVIN). Why not? You're not interested?	LINDSEY. No. Trust me. It's offensive.

STEVE (*to* LINDSEY). Of course it's *offensive* – (*Continues.*)

LINDSEY (*overlapping*). To *me*. Offensive to *me*.

STEVE. – that's the whole point of the – How? How does it offend you?

LINDSEY. Because it's disgusting and juvenile and traffics in the worst possible type of obsolete bullshit stereotypes.

Beat, then:

LENA. Well, now I *gotta* hear it.

KEVIN. No no no no no. Aww, c'mon.	STEVE. No. I can't.	LINDSEY. Not while I'm in the room.

LENA (*to* KEVIN, *re:* LINDSEY). Well, she says it's so offensive, and I have no way of knowing if she's right, and if I don't ever *hear* it, how will I ever *know*?

KEVIN *sighs, throws up his hands.*

STEVE. Um, you know what? I don't even remember it now.

LENA. Two men in jail, you said.

KATHY. Oh, *I* know this one.

LINDSEY (*a warning*). *Steven?*

LENA. Wasn't that it? Two men…

STEVE. I – Okay. So there's – *Look, it's not even my joke, okay?!!* It was told to me by Kyle Hendrickson, who, for what it's worth, happens to be –

LENA. Black.

STEVE. Right.

LENA. So the white man goes to jail.

LINDSEY (*to* STEVE). *I can't believe you actually intend to – !!* Fine.

STEVE. Anyway.

LINDSEY. Knock 'em dead.

STEVE. Goes to jail for… You know. Embezzlement. Something. Little white guy. And he's put in a jail cell with this… uhhh…

LENA. With a black man.

STEVE. Big black guy.

LINDSEY (*appalled*). And why *big?* (*Continues.*)

| STEVE (*to* LINDSEY). I am repeating, *verbatim*, a joke in the precise manner in which it was told to me. | LINDSEY. – Why does it have to be 'big'? What does that reveal about your subconscious – ? |

LENA. Little white man.

LINDSEY (*head in hands*). Oh God.

LENA. Big black man.

STEVE. In the... Yeah, so they... um, slam the cell door... behind him, I guess, and the black guy turns to the white guy, black guy goes, okay, I'm gonna give you a choice. While you're in here with me, you can either be the mommy, or you can be the daddy. And the white guy thinks for a second and he goes, uh, well, um, I guess, if it's up to *me*, then, I guess *I'd* have to say I'd prefer to be the daddy. (*Clears his throat.*) And, the black guy goes, okay, well then bend over cuz Mommy's gonna fuck you in the ass.

Long pause. No one laughs or smiles. They simply nod or shake their heads. Finally...

KATHY. That's not the one I was thinking of.

STEVE (*academically*). So: is that offensive?

LENA. No.   LINDSEY. *Are you insane??*

STEVE (*to* LINDSEY). To *you*. How is it offensive to *you*?

LINDSEY. I don't think it's *me* you should be *asking*.

LENA. No, the problem with *that* joke, see, is that it's not *funny*.

LINDSEY. No shit.

STEVE (*to* LINDSEY). *You laughed when I told it to you!!*

LENA. And had it been a *funny* joke –

STEVE. It *is* funny. Yes it is. And and and and the reason it's funny, is, is, is that it plays upon certain latent fears of – of – of – of white people, vis-à-vis the –

TOM. Okay. I'd like to add: I'm *gay*.

| STEVE. I – I – I – I – well, I didn't know that. | KATHY. See? You never know. You really don't. | LINDSEY. Nice. Nice going, Steven. Nice work. |

TOM. So I guess you think sex *between men* is funny?

STEVE. *Oh, come on!!!*

TOM. Just *inherently* funny.

STEVE. And it's not even sex, it's *rape*!

LINDSEY. So *rape* is funny.

STEVE. N – *Yes!!!* In the context of the *joke*.

KATHY. My sister was raped.

STEVE. I quit.

KATHY. So it's offensive to *me*.

LINDSEY. *And* me!

STEVE (*re:* TOM). *And* him. *And* them. *That's the point of a joke*. To permit the expression of – And what does it even *mean*, offended? I don't even know what it means.

KEVIN. How many white men does it take to change a light bulb?

TOM.	LINDSEY.	KATHY.	STEVE.
Okay, I'm about two minutes from leaving? So, heads up.	No. Can we please *not*? I'm asking you as a favour	A-ha. See? Shoe's on the other foot now.	*Fine!* Tell me the joke. I want to hear it. I do. (*Continues*.)

STEVE. How many white men *does* it take to change a light bulb?

KEVIN. All of 'em.

STEVE. And why is that?

KEVIN. One to hold the light bulb while the rest of 'em screw the entire world.

STEVE. *So?!!* You think I'm *offended*? I can do this all day. What's long and hard on a black man?

LINDSEY. *How is this happening?!!*

KEVIN. I don't know, Steve. What *is* long and hard on a black man?

STEVE. First grade. Are you offended?

KEVIN. Nope.

STEVE. Neither am I.

LINDSEY. You *can't* be offended, you *moron* – (*Continues.*)

STEVE (*overlapping, astonished laugh*). I can't?

LINDSEY. – because you've *never* been politically marginalised, unlike *the majority* of people in the world – (*Continues.*)

STEVE (*overlapping*). How can a *majority* be *marginal*?

LINDSEY. – and, by the way, *all women, everywhere,* and it's your classic white male myopia that you're blind to that basic fact.

LENA. Why is a white woman like a tampon?

All turn to LENA. *Pause.*

LINDSEY. Why is what?

LENA. It's a joke.

KEVIN. No no no no no no –

LENA. *You* told a joke, now *I'm* telling one: Why is a white woman – (*Continues.*)

KEVIN (*overlapping*). Baby, don't.

LENA (*calmly, to* KEVIN). – and please don't *baby* me. You've got three babies at *home* – (*Continues.*)

KEVIN (*overlapping, publicly*). Goodnight. I wash my hands.

LENA (*privately*). – if you need to *pacify* someone. (*To the others.*) So:

STEVE (*raising a finger*). Uhh… can you repeat the set-up?

LENA. Why…

STEVE....is a white woman, right...?

LENA....like a tampon?

> STEVE *looks around. No one else answers, so:*

STEVE. Um, I don't know, why?

LENA. Because they're both stuck up cunts.

> *Pause. Again, no one laughs or smiles.* KEVIN *shakes his head.*

LINDSEY (*even*). Wow.

LENA. But I hope you're not *offended.*

STEVE (*academically,* not *laughing*). See, *I* find that funny.

LINDSEY (*flat*). Do you?

KATHY. Well, *I'm* offended.

STEVE. *Oh, you are not.*

LINDSEY. And how does it always come back around to *the women*?

LENA (*innocently*). It was just a joke.

STEVE. *Exactly!!*

KATHY. An extremely *hostile* joke.

LINDSEY. Directed at me.

KATHY. And in what way am I *stuck-up*, exactly? You mean, because I worked my ass off putting myself through law school, that makes me *stuck-up*?

STEVE. It's a joke about a *tampon*!!

KATHY. And maybe there's a difference between being *stuck-up* and being *intelligent.*

STEVE (*to* KATHY). *You don't even know the fucking capital of Morocco!!!*

KATHY (*insulted*). Ohhhhhhh-kay.

STEVE. And you know something? If there's anyone here who's being *marginalised* by the tide of history – You don't exactly see *me* sitting in the White House, do you?

LINDSEY. *Thank the Lord*.

STEVE. But you don't see *me* wetting my pants and acting all offended.

KATHY (*to* LINDSEY, *as she packs her things*). You know, I think maybe I'm *done*.

STEVE. No. You want to know what offends *me*? How about the neighbourhood the two of us are living in right now? Bunch of white suburban assholes still driving around with the yellow-ribbon magnets on their SUVs in support of some bullshit war. *That's* the kinda shit that offends *me*.

KEVIN. Why does *that* make them assholes?

Pause.

STEVE. Why does what?

KEVIN. Said assholes have yellow ribbons on their SU –

STEVE. I didn't say that.

KEVIN. Yeah, you did, you said –

STEVE. I said *with* the magnet, not, you know, *by virtue of*.

KEVIN. So, it's not the *magnet* makes you the asshole?

LINDSEY (*to* KEVIN). You have one on your car?

KEVIN. I have three of 'em.

STEVE. Three.

KEVIN. Three.

LINDSEY. Three?

LENA. Three.

STEVE. Three.

KEVIN. One for each member of my family serving overseas.

STEVE. Great.

Pause.

KATHY. I have the pink one for breast cancer.

KEVIN. So maybe I'm a *triple* asshole, but –

LINDSEY (*fake-whisper to* KEVIN). *I think we know who the asshole is.*

STEVE. Wow.

LINDSEY (*finishing off* STEVE). Well, you're being an *idiot*. And in case you hadn't noticed, the rest of the world has begun a more sophisticated conversation about this topic than you apparently are qualified to participate in at this incredible moment in history. I mean, I used to *date* a black guy. *So what?* I mean, *seriously*. Steve. Wake up.

The same church bell that we heard in Act One begins to ring. Pause. TOM *looks at his watch.*

TOM (*claps hands together*). And it is now four o'clock.

STEVE (*privately, to* LINDSEY). When did you date a black guy?

TOM. So: final thoughts? Lena?

LENA. No.

TOM. Kev?

KEVIN. I'm good.

TOM. Anybody?

KEVIN. Very informative.

LINDSEY. Well, I want to say this: I want to say I feel angry. And I'm basically kind of hurt by the implication that's been made that, just because we want to live as your neighbours and raise a child alongside yours, that somehow, in the process of doing that, we've had our ethics called into question. Because *that* is hurtful.

LENA (*calmly*). No one has questioned your *ethics* at all.

LINDSEY. Well, I wish I could believe you.

LENA. No, what we're questioning is your *taste*.

The others rise to leave.

TOM. Kathy? I will call you
when the petition goes
through.

LINDSEY. Well, *that* was
insulting.

KATHY. Thank you.

TOM. Tuesday at the latest.

LINDSEY. Wait, what's wrong with our *taste*?

TOM (*putting on sunglasses*). Kev?

KEVIN. Right behind you.

LINDSEY. No. What is so *egregious* about the design of our
house?

KEVIN (*to* LENA, *who is about to respond*). No no no no no.
Let it go.

LENA *exits*.

KATHY (*to* LINDSEY). Sweetie, I've got a thing but I'll call
you tomorrow.

TOM (*to* LINDSEY *and* STEVE). And you guys got my
number if you want to talk?

STEVE. Yep.

*TOM is gone, with a thumbs-up. KATHY follows close
behind. At the same time, DAN enters from the kitchen
carrying a pair of bolt cutters. The others ignore him.*

KEVIN (*to* LINDSEY *and* STEVE). So, uhh… good luck with
your house. And maybe y'all can just communicate with
Tom from here on out. But, anyway, uhh… (*With a wave.*)
Y'all enjoy the rest of your evening.

*KEVIN and LENA politely exit through the open front door.
STEVE and LINDSEY stand silently for a moment, then:*

DAN (*holding up the bolt cutters*). Uhhhhh…?

LINDSEY (*quietly*). *Wow*.

STEVE. Wow is right.

LINDSEY. Amazing.

STEVE (*but not quietly enough*). And for the record? *That woman* is the cunt.

And instantly KEVIN *is back through the front door.*

KEVIN (*advancing on* STEVE). Wait a second – *what'd* you say?

All hell breaks loose.

LENA (*following* KEVIN).	KEVIN.	STEVE (*innocently*).	LINDSEY (*to* KEVIN).
Just leave it alone. Let 'em be. I don't care what kinda bullshit they think, all I want to do is go home and take the longest shower of my life.	Whaddya think I'm deaf or something? Standing right there on your front doorstep – Oh no, I *heard* you loud and clear. I'm just giving you the opportunity to repeat it to my face –	What? What? What? I didn't… Heyhey, hey, *whoa*. *Back off*, man. What is your fucking problem, dude? I didn't do anything to you or her so why can't you *chill*?	No no no no – I told you. It's the pressure. We're both under a huge amount of pressure and yes he acted like an idiot but could we all just maybe *step off*, please?

KEVIN (*in the clear*). – and when you do? I will slap the taste outta your mouth.

STEVE. Oh oh oh good, *threaten me*.

LENA. Oh, *now* you're gonna stand up for me?

KEVIN. Don't you ever insult my wife, you hear me, *bitch*?

DAN (*putting his hand on* KEVIN's *shoulder*). Hey. Let's be civilised.

KEVIN (*whirling on* DAN). Ohoho, don't you touch *me* – (*Continues.*)

| DAN. Whoa whoa whoa. That's cool. I'm just passing through, is all. | STEVE (*to* DAN). Hey, do you *mind*, okay? We happen to be having a conversation. | KEVIN. – Go putting your hands on me? Oh, no. Not in *this* neighbo – | LENA (*to* KEVIN). Oh, for God's sake, are you coming – (*Continues.*) |

LENA. – or are you too busy trying to make *friends* with everybody?

DAN *backs off and goes at the trunk with the bolt cutters as two simultaneous arguments unfold.*

LINDSEY (*to* STEVE). And why the fuck did you go and insult Kathy? We are paying her, I hope you realise?

STEVE. Yeah, well, you know what? I *agree* with them! *The house is too fucking big!*

LINDSEY. Ohhhhhhhh, do not *even* –

STEVE. Very first time we saw the plans. What did I tell you? I told you that like *fifteen times*!!

KEVIN (*to* LENA). What the hell is that supposed to – ?

LENA. Alllllllll afternoon. Always gotta be *every*body's friend. *Hi everybody! I'm Kevin!*

KEVIN (*starting to exit*). Oh gimme a fuckin' – So you want to fight with *me* now? Gotta pick a fight with *me*? You have had a bug up your ass from the moment we walked through this door .

LENA. Yeah, well, maybe some of us don't feel the

LINDSEY. Well, Steven, you're free to live wherever you want, but the baby and I will be here if you ever feel like visiting.

need to constantly *ingratiate* ourselves with everybody.

KEVIN. Well, maybe that's because some of us aren't *paranoid* and *delusional*.

KEVIN and LENA exit. By this point, DAN has succeeded in opening the trunk.

STEVE (*to* LINDSEY, *continuous from above*). Fine by me.

LINDSEY. Do you have the keys?

STEVE. I mean, God forbid my needs should ever come before the *baby's*.

LINDSEY. You really want me to choose between you and the baby?

STEVE. Oh, I'm secondary.

LINDSEY. Cuz that's an *easy* one.

STEVE. Correction: *tertiary*.

As LINDSEY *and* STEVE *continue to argue, a bespectacled young man in a military uniform descends the stairs, unnoticed and oddly out of place. This is* KENNETH, *played by the actor who played* TOM. *He carries a yellow legal pad and a transistor radio. Oblivious to the scene around him, he takes a seat by a window near the front door, as* DAN *removes a yellowed envelope from the trunk.* LINDSEY *and* STEVE *prepare to leave as their bickering continues.*

LINDSEY. Or maybe you don't *want* the baby.

STEVE. Oh! That's funny. I didn't know I had a *choice*.

LINDSEY. Oh, you had a choice.

STEVE. If only I'd *known*.

LINDSEY. And you *chose*.

STEVE. And what were the options, again? Oh that's right. A) *Let's have a baby.*

LINDSEY. Which you *chose.*

STEVE. Or B) *I'm divorcing you.*

LINDSEY. But *you* chose *A.*

STEVE. A for Arm-twisting.

LINDSEY (*going outside*). Do you have the keys?

STEVE. B for *Blackmail.*

LINDSEY (*from outside*). *Do* you have them or don't – ?

STEVE (*from the door*). *YES! YES I HAVE THE GODDAMN –* What, you think someone's gonna *rob* this place?

DAN turns to see them exit.

Help yourselves. Fuckin' shithole.

STEVE slams the door. DAN looks around with no acknowledgment of KENNETH.

DAN (*to the empty house*). Hello? Hello?

He sits on the trunk, opens the letter.

(*Reading to himself.*) Dear Mom and Dad.

Lights change. Music begins to play from KENNETH's transistor radio, not unlike the very beginning of the play. It is early morning, 1957. Dim light filters through the window, barely illuminating KENNETH. He bends over his legal pad, writing, as BEV slowly descends the stairs, dressed in her robe and slippers. She stops near the bottom.

BEV (*bleary-eyed, confused*). Kenneth?

KENNETH turns down the volume on the radio.

KENNETH. Hmm?

BEV. What are you doing down here?

KENNETH. Writing a letter.

BEV. Oh. (*Beat*.) Did your father leave already?

KENNETH (*looks outside*). I don't see the car.

BEV. What time is it?

KENNETH. Don't know.

BEV. I overslept.

KENNETH. Yup.

BEV (*yawning*). I don't know why I was up so late. I was up half the night and the house was so quiet and your father was sound asleep but for some reason my mind was just racing and it took for ever to fall asleep.

KENNETH. Go back to bed.

BEV (*finally focusing*). Oh, look how you're dressed up. Why are you all dressed up like that?

KENNETH *stares, doesn't answer.*

Kenneth?

KENNETH. Job interview.

A key turns in the front door. It opens and FRANCINE *enters in her street clothes with a scarf tied around her head. She carries a wet umbrella.*

FRANCINE (*sleepy*). Morning.

KENNETH. Morning.

BEV. Morning, Francine.

FRANCINE. Morning.

BEV. Oh, is it *raining* out there?

FRANCINE. Sprinkling a little.

BEV. I didn't even notice. Well. It's good for the grass.

She stands at the bottom of the stairs, as FRANCINE *crosses past her and up the hallway.* BEV *hesitates.*

KENNETH. Aren't you going back to sleep?

BEV (*pensive*). Oh, I will. I'm just about to.

For a moment, she stares into space, then turns to
KENNETH.

But you know, I think things are about to change. I really do.
I know it's been a hard couple of years for all of us, I know
they have been, but I really believe things are about to
change for the better. I firmly believe that.

KENNETH *waits.* BEV *turns and starts back up the stairs.*

You have enough light, there?

KENNETH. Uh-huh.

BEV (*as she ascends*). Well, don't hurt your eyes.

She is gone. KENNETH *turns the radio back up, resumes
writing.* DAN *continues to read. The lights slowly fade as
the music concludes.*

The End.